DETECTING THE FAKES

A COLLECTOR'S GUIDE TO THIRD REICH MILITARIA

DETECTING THE FAKES

ROBIN LUMSDEN

LONDON

IAN ALLAN LTD

New York

HIPPOCRENE BOOKS

Cover photography by
Alan Lauder/Norval (Photographers) Ltd

Above photograph courtesy
A. Romanes & Sons Ltd.

Published in the United States by
HIPPOCRENE BOOKS, Inc.,
171 Madison Avenue,
New York, N.Y. 10016
ISBN 0-7818-0324-1

First published 1989
Reprinted 1992
Third impression 1994
ISBN 0 7110 1868 5

Published in the UK by Ian Allan, Ltd, Shepperton, Surrey.

Printed in the United States of America.

Also by Robin Lumsden:
A COLLECTOR'S GUIDE TO
THIRD REICH MILITARIA
8½″ x 5¾″   192pp paperback

This companion volume is a compact
but comprehensive guide to the full
range of Third Reich militaria.
Illustrated with over 180 photographs
and 15 line drawings, the book explores
each of the main specialist areas and
provides notes on their manufacture
and their preservation and display.

Contents

Introduction

The antiques trade has for long had to suffer an influx of reproductions and copies of virtually everything that is considered rare or valuable, but no field of collecting has ever been so saturated by fakes as Third Reich militaria is today. The collecting of Nazi regalia began amongst advancing Allied soldiers before 1945, and during the 1950s and 1960s such was the worldwide demand for all types of Third Reich items that several dealers began to have it crudely reproduced and passed their fakes off as genuine articles, often at great profit. The 1970s and 1980s witnessed an even bigger boom in the creation of improved fakes to meet an ever-increasing demand.

When my book, *A Collector's Guide to Third Reich Militaria*, was published by Ian Allan Ltd in 1987, it was generally greeted with some approbation as a handy reference work summarising the entire range of subject matter 'from scratch', something which had never been done before. Yet while it included sections describing all the main specialist areas of the hobby, restoration, preservation, values and a list of dealers — as well as a fairly comprehensive glossary and bibliography — by far the most enthusiastic response was prompted by the hints given on reproduction identification. These were in a verbal form only, since all the photographs used in the book were of original items.

This companion volume is a direct result of that response. Readers will see that I have again devoted a section to each of the main specialist areas of Third Reich collecting, as methods of fake detection obviously vary depending on whether the particular item under consideration is a badge, dagger, peaked cap or whatever. Each section describes the differences between originals and copies, and these descriptions are backed up by illustrations showing a wide range of reproductions of both good and poor quality, often in direct comparison to their genuine counterparts. New fakes are constantly being devised and old ones improved upon and it would be impossible to cover all reproductions in existence. However, by covering a representative selection, and in the belief that 'a picture speaks a thousand words', I hope to convey to readers the idea that there is, in the majority of cases, a way to identify not only a copy from an original, but also one type of reproduction from another and one genuine maker's variant from another. It has not been my intention to reiterate the histories behind the various awards, tunics and other items illustrated as that ground was covered in *A Collector's Guide to Third Reich Militaria*. This book, either as a companion volume or as a reference in its own right, is devoted entirely to the subject of fake detection and presupposes in the reader at least a working knowledge of Nazi/collector terminology and abbreviations.

This work is a 'first' in its field and, therefore, is based entirely upon personal experience built up over 20 years of collecting. As a young collector, like any other, I was duped on occasion by the fake merchants. This reinforced my belief, still held, that all copies are 'bad' and should have no place in a serious collection, even as space-fillers. Having said that, there now exists a legitimate market in the selling of reproductions and, as the supply of choice original material continually dwindles, there is emerging a fraternity of collectors who cannot, or choose not to, afford the now increasing prices necessary to engage upon a collection of genuine artefacts. Their interest lies in the visual appearance of, rather than the history behind, the pieces they possess and this allows them to collect replicas in much the same way as others buy prints instead of original oil paintings. These collectors may feel confident that they have obtained reasonable value for money. Their purchases, however, will remain static in value and so never prove to be investments. More importantly, they will never be quite equal to the originals, either in quality or from a historical standpoint. Despite the fact that such an open and straightforward market in reproductions has developed, a number of dealers still perceive the need to peddle their fakes as genuine items, which they do at enormous profit. Excellent reproductions of Juncker-made ('L/12') Knight's Crosses, for example, imported into the UK in 1987 for sale as copies at £40 each, were soon being passed off as originals at the 'bargain' price of £750!

Contrary to popular belief, not all antique dealers are experts in their subject. It is true to say that they, like collectors, do get caught out by fakes from time to time. An Edinburgh dealer friend recently called to show me a new acquisition of his — a 'presentation dagger'. The item in question was a standard early 1933-pattern SA dagger but with a superb quality acid-etched artificial damascus blade by P. D. Lüneschloss of Solingen. The reverse of the blade bore a raised gilded Ernst Röhm dedication. Upon examination I concluded that the blade was a modern replacement, basing my finding upon the following points: Röhm blades were never of the damascus or etched damascus type; Lüneschloss was not one of the original authorised makers of Röhm blades; the particular Lüneschloss mark featured was the one used by the factory after 1945; the blade had slightly uneven edges, indicating regrinding; and the reverse crossguard had the Gruppe mark for Westfalen, presentation daggers never being Gruppe marked. I advised the dealer that, discarding the fake blade, the rest of the dagger would be worth about £50 as spare parts. He sheepishly admitted that he had paid a complete stranger £800 for it at an arms fair in the belief that it was an original honour dagger, valued at around £2,500 and had hoped to re-sell it as such. This tale amply illustrates the point that any dealer's guarantee of authenticity, however well-intentioned, may prove to be worthless. As

my friend found out to his cost, the buyer will always be the loser at the end of the day if he does not know his facts prior to purchase.

So what can the collector do to ensure that what he is getting is the real thing? Firstly, he should try to visit as many military museums, militaria shops and antique fairs as possible, so as to view items on display and get their 'feel'. Secondly, he should not be afraid to ask! Most dealers are honest individuals and by asking if a piece is authentic the dealer is obliged to make his position clear. Even if he is genuinely uncertain, he can express an opinion. At that point, of course, the onus of satisfaction again returns to the buyer, for even among experts there will invariably be patches of disagreement or contention. When the dealer states that a piece or a repair is 'contemporary', does he mean 'contemporary to then' or 'contemporary to now'? Does 'distressed' in his catalogue signify 'naturally aged' or 'artificially aged'? Does 'restored' denote 'restored with original parts' or 'restored with reproduction parts'? The collector must never be reticent in asking for clarification of such ambiguous terminology, which frequently appears in sales lists. Even where a money-back guarantee is offered, pre-purchase queries like these can save much inconvenience later on.

The 'sharks' among dealers, those who wilfully and knowingly pass fakes as originals, are not liked by other dealers. They bring the trade a bad name, they cast the shadow of doubt upon their fellows, and so they make enemies. There is a world of difference between a dealer who deliberately defrauds the public and one who errs in judgement concerning authenticity. The collector is advised that his most secure prospect is to study his subject thoroughly. This is not idle research, because a true enthusiast will appreciate his subject for all its academic benefits and material failings and not simply for the high prices that the subject matter brings. In fact, if it were not for the financial gains, there would be no point in engaging in faking at all. Every collector would be wise to bear that in mind, for if he is prepared to spend large amounts of cash then he had better know what he is buying. As the saying goes, 'fools and their money are easily parted'. Everybody makes the odd mistake, but too many Third Reich enthusiasts have had to endure the horrible sinking feeling suffered when their unfortunate purchases have been revealed for what they really are. Considerable investments have been lost through too much reliance having been placed on knowledge gleaned from large textbooks which describe the history behind certain collectables in great detail at the expense of omitting coverage of even the most elementary methods of fake detection. It is my earnest hope that this book will prevent at least a few readers from being so defrauded, disappointed and embarrassed.

Photographs credited 'IWM' are reproduced by kind permission of the Trustees of the Imperial War Museum, London. All other photographs were taken by Alan Lauder of Norval (Photographers) Ltd, Dunfermline, Fife, whose skilful assistance I gratefully acknowledge.

Cairneyhill   *Robin Lumsden*
March 1989

1 Orders and Decorations

Medals and awards of all countries and periods have long been the subject of reproduction, but none more so than those of Nazi Germany. From the infancy of the Third Reich, Hitler set about creating an entirely new range of very attractive national orders and decorations, and this process continued right up to the final weeks of World War 2. Nazi decorations are now the most popular and expensive specialist area in the field of Third Reich collecting and, consequently, have been the subject of the most extensive faking. All awards which existed under Hitler (and a few which never did!) have been reproduced. Some fakes, cold cast by local dealers using basic plaster moulds, would fool no-one. Others, struck from original dies by firms authorised to manufacture decorations under the Third Reich, are near perfect. This section will describe and illustrate a selection of originals and copies, and discuss the various points to be considered when attempting to determine authenticity.

The 1939 Iron Cross has undoubtedly suffered more faking than any other decoration in the world, due to the fact that examples are constantly being sought after by collectors both of Nazi awards and of medals in general. During World War 2, Iron Crosses were made by well over 30 different manufacturers, but all of these firms used master dies produced by just one company, Steinhauer & Lück of Lüdenscheid, whose senior engraver, Hans Escher, designed the 1939 Iron Cross. This ensured that all genuine pieces, irrespective of maker, conformed to a single ideal, with perfect detailing and a 'high' swastika which was level with the crisply beaded rim.

The lowest grade, the Iron Cross Second Class, measured 44mm in diameter and was made in three parts: a core, an obverse rim and a reverse rim. The core was normally die-stamped iron sheeting, trimmed, sand-blasted then covered with a matt black oil-based lacquer and oven baked in a process known as stove enamelling. The rims were die-stamped from German silver (also known as 'Neusilber' or Nickel Silver). The blackened core was placed between the rims which were then soldered together, their outer edges being smoothed by hand polishing. The rim beading was thereafter frosted and the flanges burnished and the entire rim was then coated with a protective transparent lacquer. Finally, a suspension ring was attached and often stamped with the manufacturer's code number. Apart from a few pieces produced with blackened brass, copper or zinc cores, for use by naval personnel whose iron-cored crosses tended to rust after weeks at sea, all original Second Class Iron Crosses were made in this way.

Genuine examples of the Iron Cross Second Class are still readily available at low prices, so fakes produced have tended to be of the one-piece film prop variety, such as that shown in **Plate 1,** which is not really intended to deceive anyone.

The Iron Cross First Class was made in the same way as the Second Class, but with the plain reverse sand-blasted and matt silver plated. It was normally attached to the pocket by means of a wide, thick, tapering, blunt-ended pin bar, but recipients could purchase official copies with screw-back devices if they so wished. This latter type had a retaining head protruding from the rear of the cross which was pushed through a hole in the tunic pocket and was then fixed in place by a round plate and threaded pin screwed on from behind the pocket. Screw-back crosses were less likely to become detached in action and were frequently bent to a convex shape to improve fit, despite the fact that the manufacture of convex Iron Crosses was forbidden in September 1940. A small hook on the reverse upper arm prevented the screw-back cross from swivelling around on the tunic pocket. Some First Class crosses featured hollow alloy cores making them lighter to wear and easier to bend into a convex shape if desired. Again, the manufacturer's code number often appeared on the cross, stamped on either the pin bar or the reverse lower arm.

The earliest fakes of the Iron Cross First Class were cast in the 1950s from a soft lead-based alloy which could easily be twisted out of shape by mere finger pressure. Roughly painted and featuring a thin needle pin, they were passed off as having been produced from lead 'due to the acute shortage of iron and nickel silver in Germany towards the end of the war'. Similar cast copies were made as film props in the 1960s from a brittle alloy which snapped under pressure. The latest reproductions are nicely die-struck, but are let down by the fact that they comprise a single piece of metal only, not having separate core and rims. **Plates 2** and **3** illustrate original and fake First Class Iron Crosses.

The next highest grade, the Knight's Cross of the Iron Cross, retained the same basic design and manner of construction as the Iron Cross Second Class, but measured 48mm across. The frame was made of real silver, which could vary in purity from 80% to 93.5%, and each cross was stamped accordingly on the reverse upper rim with the continental silver hallmark ranging from '800' to '935'. The suspension loop was similarly hallmarked. The maker's code number occasionally featured alongside the frame hallmark. Presentation pieces were all in '800' silver and were manufactured by three firms only: Steinhauer & Lück of Lüdenscheid, Deschler & Sohn of Munich, and C. E. Juncker of Berlin. Crosses produced by the Lüdenscheid firm were stamped solely with the '800' hallmark, while those made after 1941 by Deschler and Juncker had the '800' frame hallmark accompanied by the firms' code numbers '1' and 'L/12' respectively. These presentation pieces were always of superb quality, with high swastikas and dates having sharp, well defined edges. The rims were finely soldered together and hand-finished so as to leave only a hairline trace of the join, with no spaces, and the core fitted perfectly between them. An insignificant number of 'duplicate' copies for private purchase by recipients were made with frames in '935' silver by the firms of C. F. Zimmermann and Otto Schickle, both of Pforzheim, and Klein & Quenzer of Idar-Oberstein, but production of these items for open sale was forbidden in 1941. Few recipients ever bothered to acquire extra crosses for front-line or dress wear in any case. During the 1944-45 period issue Knight's Crosses began to appear with zinc cores and nickel silver frames, yet details on such 'ersatz' crosses were still well defined and a high quality appearance was maintained.

Most reproductions of the Knight's Cross are easily detected, being of the one-piece die-struck type in soft lead-based or brittle glittery alloys (see **Plates 4** and **5**). In the 1960s and 1970s, good quality fakes were constructed in the correct three-piece manner by the firm of Rudolf Souval, Vienna, but they lacked the overall quality of the genuine article. In particular, the swastika was too low, not being level with the beaded edge, and the frame, although stamped '800', was in lightweight silver plate rather than real silver. Moreover, the soldering of the obverse and reverse rims was never perfected by Souval, resulting in ugly spaces along the edges and poor fitting of the core, while the beading itself was a bit blurred and lacked crispness in places. The latest fakes of the Knight's Cross were produced in Denmark in 1987 and have since been a cause of great concern to the collecting fraternity, for they are almost perfect copies of the Juncker-made originals, even down to the 'L/12' mark. They were imported into the UK by a well-known dealer, complete with

modern ribbons and presentation cases, for legitimate sale to collectors as good quality reproductions at £40 apiece. However, needless to say, it was not long before most were snapped up by a few disreputable persons who then re-sold them as originals at the 'bargain price' of £750 each! The suspension loops on these fakes have roughly clipped, sharp ends as opposed to the smoothly rounded ends characteristic of originals. The only other means of distinguishing them from genuine Junckermade crosses are the form of the ring or eye on the upper arm and the size of the 'L/12' mark. These indicators are described in **Fig 1.**

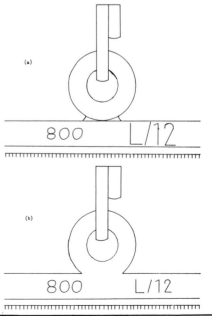

Fig 1 *Drawing (a), above, indicates the reverse upper arm characteristics of original Knight's Crosses produced by the firm of C. E. Juncker, Berlin. Note that the ring or eye which accommodates the suspension loop is a separate item, attached by silver solder to the top of the cross. The firm's code number 'L/12' is noticeably bigger than the '800' silver mark. Drawing (b), below, shows the fake counterpart. It has the ring or eye as an integral part of the rim stamping, which was correct for Steinhauer & Lück and Deschler originals, but not for Juncker-made pieces. The 'L/12' on the reproduction is no larger than the '800' mark.*

13

Plate 1 Iron Cross Second Class: *original (left) and reproduction (right). The original is made of three parts, viz an iron centre and German silver obverse and reverse rims soldered together. Detailing on the rim beading is crisp. The swastika measure 11mm from tip to tip and the suspension ring is stamped with the manufacturer's code number '125' (Eugen Gauss, Pforzheim). The reproduction is a single-piece die-stamping in a brittle, glittery alloy. Overall quality is fairly good, but the beading is less detailed with fewer lines (20 on each straight edge, as opposed to 30 on the original). The swastika measures only 9.5mm across and the eye on the top of the cross, which is an integral part of the stamping, has had to be twisted through 90° to accommodate the suspension ring in the correct manner.*

Plate 2 Iron Cross First Class: *original (above) and two reproductions (lower left and right). The original comprises three parts, ie an iron core sandwiched between an obverse rim and a flat reverse, both in German silver. Details are perfectly defined and the swastika is the same height as the rim beading. The fake on the lower left is a single-piece casting in lead, produced in a Gloucester dealer's workshop as a film or stage prop. Quality is very poor, with almost no definition to the beaded edge and a gloss black hand-painted finish. The swastika is too low. This item can be bent easily by mere finger pressure, although similar crosses have been cast in a brittle alloy which readily snaps when pressurised. The copy on the lower right is expertly made with high swastika and well defined beading. The rim has a frosted appearance which was characteristic of originals when new. There is little doubt that this reproduction, when compared to the previously described fake, might be accepted as genuine. However, it is let down by the fact that it is a one-piece striking. Moreover, the date '1939' takes a much plainer form than that on the original.*

Plate 3 *Reverses of the items shown in* **Plate 2.** *The original (above) displays the typical broad, thick, tapering, blunt-ended pin bar. The cast fake (lower left) has a very thin, unstable needle pin, never used on genuine Iron Crosses. Note also the rough finish with pock marks characteristic of a poor casting technique. The copy on the lower right is far more convincing, with a semi-broad pointed pin bar and wide clip identical to that currently used on awards by the Federal Republic of West Germany. The pin bar is crudely stamped 'L/17', the wartime code number for the firm of Hermann Wernstein, Jena-Löbstadt.*

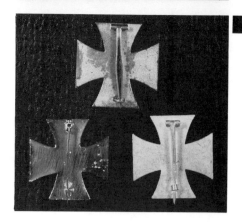

Plate 4 Knight's Cross of the Iron Cross: *original (above) and fake (below). The original is in the usual three parts with superb detailing. The swastika is high, ie the same height as the rim beading, is 13mm from point to point, and has razor-sharp edges. The rim is in '800' silver, as is the suspension loop which is of substantial quality with perfectly rounded ends. The ribbon measures 45mm across. The fake is a single piece die-stamping in a brittle alloy. The swastika measures just 9.5mm across and the suspension loop is simply a paper clip! The ribbon is only 38mm wide.*

Plate 5 *Edges of original (above) and fake (below) Knight's Crosses. The original has 35 well-defined lines to the beaded edge and the obverse and reverse rims are soldered together and hand finished to leave only a smooth trace of the hairline join. The reproduction has 26 poorly-defined lines to the beaded edge. Its one-piece rim still bears the rough marks caused by the die-stamping process.*

15

Plate 6 *Oakleaves and Swords (left) and Oakleaves, Swords and Diamonds (right) to the Knight's Cross. Both items were produced after 1957 by the firm of Steinhauer & Lück of Lüdenscheid, as part of their range of de-Nazified decorations for wear by World War 2 veterans. Far more were made than were ever required, however, and thousands of surplus pieces were offered for sale to collectors at very cheap prices. The item on the left is die-stamped from a white metal alloy, with rough edges. That on the right is made from the same material but is silver plated and has crisper definition. The 24 'diamonds' on the latter are, in fact, pieces of glass. Note that the upper sword hilts are tangent to the blades in both cases: on originals, the hilts never touched the blades.*

Plate 7 *Reverses of items shown in* **Plate 6.** *The piece on the left is concave and unmarked while that on the right is flat and hallmarked '800', although it is only silver plated. The suspension loops on both have roughly clipped, sharp ends as opposed to the smoothly rounded ends characteristic of originals. The swords have unfinished reverses, typical of Steinhauer & Lück manufacture. It is worthy of note that all genuine examples of the Oakleaves, Swords and Diamonds were hand crafted by jewellers and were hollow-backed so as to enhance the brilliance of the stones.*

Plate 8 *1939 Bar to the 1914 Iron Cross Second Class: original (left) and reproduction (right). The original is crisply die-stamped from German silver. The reproduction is cast in a brittle, white metal alloy. Note that the fake eagle's left wing is deformed due to a casting flaw.*

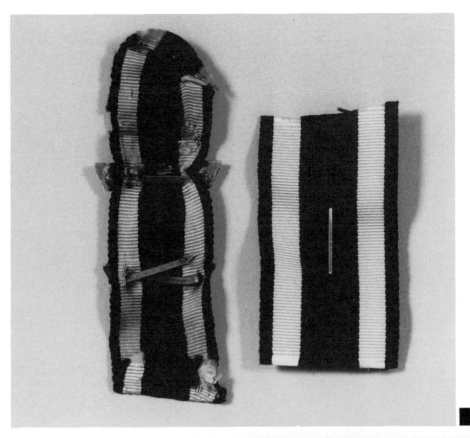

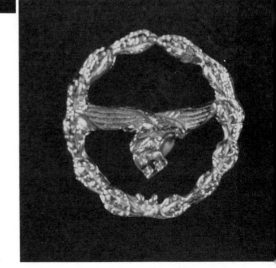

Plate 9 *Reverses of items shown in* **Plate 8**. *The original (left) is attached to its ribbon by four bent prongs, whereas the copy (right) features a needle pin.*

Plate 10 Fake Luftwaffe Roll of Honour Clasp: *crudely cast in solid brass with a very flat appearance and a stick-pin attachment to the rear.*

17

Wartime presentation examples of the Oakleaf cluster to the Knight's Cross were crisply die-struck in real silver by two manufacturers only: Steinhauer & Lück of Lüdenscheid and Gebrüder Godet & Co of Berlin. The reverse of each piece was smooth and slightly concave, with a heavy round-ended suspension loop neatly silver-soldered into position. Oakleaves produced by Steinhauer & Lück were stamped on the reverse with the '800' hallmark, while those made by Godet bore one of the hallmarks '900' or '935' accompanied by either of the company's two code marks, '21' or 'L/50'. Original Oakleaves suspension loops were never hallmarked.

Fakes of the Oakleaves are most commonly cast from a soft lead-based alloy or die-stamped in silver plated brass with a hollow reverse. They usually have a spurious '800' hallmark on the suspension loop. After 1957, Steinhauer & Lück officially reproduced the cluster as part of their range of de-Nazified decorations for wear by veterans. These copies were struck using the original dies and came in two forms: a white metal alloy type with an unmarked concave reverse; and a silver plated version with a flat reverse hallmarked '800'. Both are rather rough around the edges and have poorly finished clipped suspension loops with sharp ends.

The original Oakleaves and Swords to the Knight's Cross comprised a device identical to the Oakleaf cluster but with a longer suspension loop and the addition of two crossed silver swords, in a single die striking, soldered below. Those examples produced by Steinhauer & Lück had plain sword backs while Godet pieces had the reverse of the swords detailed as per the obverse. In both cases, however, the upper sword hilts were separated from the blades above.

Postwar fakes of the Oakleaves and Swords, like those of the Oakleaves, are usually in soft lead-based alloy or hollow silver plated brass with the swords forming an integral part of the casting or stamping. On most of these counterfeits, the space between the base of the Oakleaves and the crossed swords is solid, and the suspension loop is spuriously hallmarked. Official post-1957 Steinhauer & Lück reproductions are identical to their post-1957 Oakleaves

already described, but with the addition of crossed swords. These swords have the same plain reverse as their wartime counterparts, but the upper sword hilts are now tangent to the blades above. It would appear, therefore, that the original pre-1945 sword dies used by Steinhauer & Lück were not available in 1957, necessitating the manufacture of slightly inaccurate replacements.

The Oakleaves, Swords and Diamonds to the Knight's Cross, often referred to simply as 'the Diamonds', was die-struck in several parts from platinum, white gold or silver and hand-finished by selected jewellers, notably Klein of Berlin. Consequently, no two examples were identical. The presentation set was slightly larger and more elongated in shape than the standard Oakleaves and Swords and quality was exquisite. Encrusted with diamonds of different sizes, varying from 24 to 53 in number, it had a hollow reverse to enhance the brilliance of the stones. Each recipient was presented also with a duplicate set for everyday wear and such regulation copies, although still well made in hollow silver, were inferior in construction, having imitation diamonds. The 'Diamonds' award has not been seriously copied because of the expense involved, although Steinhauer & Lück enhanced a few of their post-1957 Oakleaves and Swords by adding pieces of cut glass to them to make 'Diamonds' for museum display purposes.

Post-1957 Steinhauer & Lück productions of the Oakleaves and Swords, and Oakleaves, Swords and Diamonds, are illustrated in **Plates 6** and **7**. They are the best copies of these awards currently on the market and the ones most likely to fool collectors.

The senior grades of the Iron Cross, namely the Golden Oakleaves, Swords and Diamonds, the Grand Cross, and the Star to the Grand Cross, have not been the subject of serious reproduction since all originals are so rare as to be individually accounted for. A large number of one-piece cast copies of the Grand Cross exist, but they are crude in the extreme and could never pass as the real thing.

The 1939 Bars to the 1914 Iron Cross First and Second Classes were initially die-struck from German silver or high quality silver plated white metal with a frosted finish and mirror highlights. From 1942, zinc was used in their construction. Zinc bars were coated with a white wash or silver paint which soon wore off, leaving the dull grey base colour. However, even the latest wartime bars were well defined and difficult to bend.

Reproductions of the Second Class Bar are usually cast in soft lead-based or brittle white alloys, with rough detailing and a thin needle pin on the reverse instead of the correct four prongs (see **Plates 8** and **9**). The 27mm 'Prinzen' bar has not been copied. Fakes of the First Class Bar are similar in style to those of the Second Class and, again, feature a thin unstable needle pin rather than the wide pin bar, standard needle pin or screw-back device which were characteristic of original variants.

The three forms of Roll of Honour Clasp instituted in 1944 for the army/Waffen-SS, navy and Luftwaffe, which were worn through the second buttonhole of the tunic attached to a piece of 1939 Iron Cross Second Class ribbon, were always die-stamped in high relief from a zinc-based alloy, gold plated with polished highlights. Each had a hollow reverse with four flat prongs or round pins for affixing to the ribbon. A few army/Waffen-SS clasps comprised two parts (ie swastika and wreath) soldered together, but the majority were single-piece die-strikings.

Reproductions of the Roll of Honour Clasp are all very flat and solid, cast in brass or a brittle white alloy. Some have a single needle pin on the reverse and others a stick-pin attachment. The army/Waffen-SS version has a deformed ribbon bow to the wreath and a crudely painted black swastika, whilst the naval fake has the ring at the top of the anchor and the area between the bottom of the anchor and the wreath pierced out; originals had these parts solid. The Luftwaffe reproduction (see **Plate 10**) lacks curvature in the wings of the eagle.

THE WAR ORDER OF THE GERMAN CROSS

The War Order of the German Cross was one of the most impressive of all Third Reich awards and its value in recent years has risen dramatically. As a result, it has been widely reproduced for the collector market.

Both silver and gold divisions of the original German Cross were convex and expertly constructed in five main die-struck sections: a 63mm silver-plated brass backplate; a grey-painted fluted brass plate of 'sunburst' design; a silver plated and red enamelled tombak disc; a gilded or silvered brass laurel wreath; and a 21mm silver plated and black enamelled tombak swastika. The swastika had two prongs on its reverse which attached to the disc and all other parts were held together by four brass rivets which extended from the wreath to the rear of the back-plate. The reverse showed the rivet heads which were normally of the solid domed type, although a few originals had ring-ended rivets, with smooth raised edges and hollow centres. A broad, thick, tapering, blunt-ended pin bar was attached to the rear for affixing to the tunic and usually bore the maker's code number. The principal producers of the award were Deschler of Munich ('1' or 'L/10'), Steinhauer & Lück of Lüdenscheid ('4' or 'L/16'), and C. F. Zimmermann of Pforzheim ('20' or 'L/52').

The German Cross was a prestige award and all original examples were made in the above manner. Unlike many other Nazi decorations, its plated and enamelled brass and tombak features were never superceded by zinc and paint. A few variants were produced with six rivets rather than four, and some holders had their awards altered by local jewellers to replace the pin bar by a screw-back device, but these were rare exceptions. Reproductions of the German Cross fall into four main categories, as follows:

(i) Single-piece castings in white metal alloy, with thin needle pins. These items are often painted in the appropriate colours and used as film props. **Plates 11** and **12** show one such copy alongside an original cased German Cross in Gold.

Plate 11 War Order of the German Cross in Gold: original (left) and fake (right). The convex original, which is in its correct case, is expertly constructed in five parts: a 63mm silver plated brass back-plate; a grey painted fluted brass plate; a silver plated and red enamelled tombak disc; a gilded brass laurel wreath; and a 21mm silver plated and black enamelled tombak swastika. The swastika has two prongs on its reverse which attach it to the disc, and all other parts are held together by four solid domed rivets which extend from the wreath to the rear of the back-plate. The fake (right) is a flat, single-piece casting produced by a Gloucester dealer as a film or stage prop. The swastika has been crudely painted black, and the remainder of the item would also be hand painted prior to delivery to the film or theatrical company. This type of fake is not intended to deceive anyone.

Plate 12 Reverses of items shown in **Plate 11**. Note the heavy pin bar and rivets on the original (left) as opposed to the needle pin and absence of rivets on the film prop. The underside of the pin bar on the original bears the code mark '20', denoting manufacture by C. F. Zimmermann of Pforzheim.

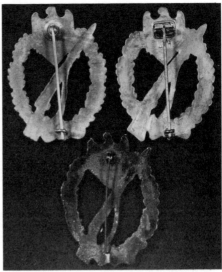

Plate 13 Infantry Assault Badge: *originals (above) and reproduction (below).* The original at upper left is die-struck zinc with a silver plating while that at upper right is heavier die-struck kriegsmetall with a white wash. Both are convex and measure 46mm across. However, they display slight differences in detail attributable to manufacturers' variations. Note, for example, that the area behind the rifle bolt is pierced out on the badge on the left but is solid on that on the right. The reproduction (below) is crudely cast in a tombak-based alloy, is flat in appearance with poor definition, and measures 44mm across.

Plate 14 *Reverses of items shown in* **Plate 13**. *The original at upper left is unmarked and has a needle pin with a ball hinge, while that at upper right is marked 'W. H.' (Walter & Henlein, Gablonz) and features a needle pin with standard hinge. The fake (below) bears the thin needle pin and pock-marked finish characteristic of a poor quality casting.*

Plate 15 General Assault Badge: *originals (above) and reproduction (below). The original at upper left is cast, bare zinc while that at upper right is die-struck zinc with a silver plating. Note small differences in detail, particularly to the eagle's head and body and in definition of the oakleaves. The reproduction (below) is crudely cast in a brittle alloy.*

(ii) Five-piece castings, poor in detail, with the components glued together. These sometimes feature four false rivet heads glued to the reverse.

(iii) Five-piece rivetted die-strikings of very good quality, but flat in form, not convex, and with only three rivets. The pin bars on these fakes are very thin, like narrow knife blades.

(iv) Five-piece convex items of excellent quality produced by the firm of Rudolf Souval, Vienna, using original dies. The components are rivetted in the correct manner, but the parts are loose fitting and the rivets are of a cheap hollow tombak variety with rough edges. All feature Souval's typical semi-broad pointed pin bar and retaining clip, the latter comprising simply a circular piece of sheet metal with a central strip cut out and bent over to retain the pin.

Souval's early back-plates were cast rather than die-struck, with a lack of crisp detail to the points of the star, some of which were missing altogether.

The private purchase active service version of the German Cross was hand-embroidered in cotton, silk and aluminium threads on a woollen base appropriate in colour to the tunic on which it was to be worn. The metal laurel wreath was much lighter than that on the presentation award, being hollow stamped zinc alloy with a polished gold or silver plating and four prongs on the rear for attachment. Reproductions, which are often embroidered on felt bases, are very crude with poor stitching and ill-formed swastikas. The fake metal wreath is either of solid brass or lead-based alloy and lacks the fine detail of the original, particularly around the date '1941'.

THE WAR BADGE

For many years, dealers have offered reproduction Nazi war badges for sale. The quality of these pieces varies considerably, from the excellent copies struck by Rudolf Souval of Vienna in the 1970s and 1980s using original dies, to the crude cast fakes turned out by the thousand in dealers' workshops all over the world. The flood of reproductions has had the unfortunate effect of making many collectors lose confidence in war badges, automatically assuming that any reasonably priced item must be faked. This has helped push up the price of the scarcer of the genuine pieces to a point beyond the reach of the average collector. Many enthusiasts still rely on evidence of age and wear as being sure signs of authenticity but they forget that aluminium, used in the manufacture of many types of original Nazi badges, never accumulates a distinctive patina and that sandpaper and acid treatments can artificially age a piece 50 years in as many seconds. A 'weathered' look to an item is certainly a good sign, but several other points need to be considered before a firm decision as to originality can be made. For example, is the quality of finish good enough? Are the proper metals used? Are the markings correct? Are there markings on a badge which should not have them? Is the pin assembly right? Is the badge one which was designed and instituted but never, in fact, produced during the Third Reich? These points will be expanded upon in the following pages.

From the outset, it must be understood that original war badges were produced by many different firms. They could be solid or hollow-backed and were both die-struck and cast. The earliest awards were manufactured in aluminium but this medium, tried and tested so far as uniform accoutrements were concerned, was deemed to be too flimsy for the making of national decorations. It was soon dropped and between 1937 and 1942 war badges and the closely related qualification badges were made variously from bronze (an alloy of copper and tin), brass (an alloy of copper and zinc), German silver (an alloy of copper, zinc and nickel), and tombakbronze or 'tombak' (an alloy of copper, zinc and tin). These badges were heavily plated in the appropriate colours. With new metal restrictions, 1942 saw the widespread introduction of greyish zinc-

Fig 2 Genuine War Badge Pin Assemblies: *a selection of pin assemblies which feature on original war badges.*

(a) *Standard hinge, needle pin and clip. Used on all types of war badge.*

(b) *Barrel hinge; standard needle pin and clip. Most commonly used on Luftwaffe awards.*

(c) *Ball hinge; standard needle pin; retaining clip soldered into hole in reverse of badge. A variation preferred by a small number of manufacturers.*

(d) *Hinge cast into reverse of badge; standard needle pin; clip cast into reverse of badge. Featured on mid-late war cast pieces, particularly by Assmann.*

(e) *Solid hinge; broad, thick, tapering, blunt-ended pin bar; heavy clip soldered directly to badge reverse.*

(f) *As (e), but with two-part clip, the hook being soldered to a circular base which is in turn soldered to the badge reverse.*

(g) *As (f), but with hinge and clip set into recesses in the badge reverse. Characteristic of awards made by Josef Feix & Söhne, Gablonz.*

(h) *Hinge cast into badge; broad, tapering pin bar is fluted; retaining clip soldered into hole in reverse of badge. Type of assembly used by Schwerin of Berlin on their U-Boat Combat Clasp.*

Types (e)–(g) are most commonly found on naval war badges and on combat and flight clasps. When a horizontal pin arrangement was used on naval war badges, a top hook was also added for stability.

based alloys in the manufacture of war badges. Such badges were given a coloured 'wash' or 'dip', or were even hand-painted, but they soon reverted to their base grey as the colour wore off. The standard of zinc alloys declined as the war progressed, culminating in the poor quality 'kriegs-metall', an alloy of copper, zinc and lead. However, details always remained well defined and none of these genuine badges could be bent without considerable pressure.

In the normal case, the war badge was struck or cast in one piece of metal, but

Fig 3 Fake War Badge Pin Assemblies: *a selection of pin assemblies which feature on reproduction war badges.*

(a) *Hinge cast into rear of badge as integral part; very thin needle pin; very thin, unstable retaining clip.*

(b) *Crude hinge; very thin needle pin; unstable clip. Normally found on the rough film prop fakes produced in Gloucester.*

(c) *As (b), but with the added refinement of a Souval-type clip.*

(d) *Correct standard hinge and needle pin, but with a Souval-type clip.*

(e) *Souval-type semi-broad, semi-thick, sharp-ended pin bar and retaining clip.*

(f) *As (e), but with standard retaining clip. This is the latest and most convincing of all the fake pin assemblies and is the variety currently used on West German awards.*

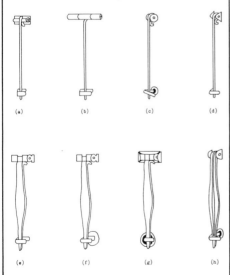

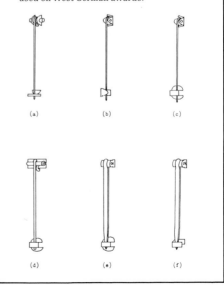

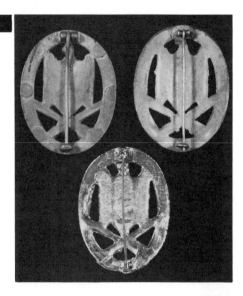

Plate 16 *Reverses of items shown in* **Plate 15**. *The original at upper left has a standard needle pin. The hinge and clip form integral parts of the overall casting. Note the six circular raised pads which mark the points where the ejector pins pushed the badge out of the casting mould. This item bears the 'A' mark of F. W. Assmann & Söhne, Lüdenscheid. The original at upper right is unmarked. Its hinge and clip are set into recesses in the badge. The cast fake (below) compares poorly to the original Assmann casting.*

Plate 17 Tank Battle Badge: *original (left) and fake (right). The original is die-stamped zinc with a silver wash while the fake is cast in a tombak-based alloy. Detail on the copy is excellent and it compares very well with the original. It would undoubtedly fool many collectors.*

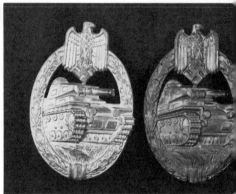

Plate 18 *Reverses of items shown in* **Plate 17**. *The original (left) is solid with a standard needle pin and bears the 'HA' mark of Hermann Aurich, Dresden. The fake (right) is hollow and has apparently been cast from a hollow Assmann original as it features the company's 'A' mark above the tank wheels on the lower right. The only real give-away with this reproduction, which was purchased direct from the Gloucester manufacturer, is the thin needle pin typical of his copies.*

Plate 19 Anti-Partisan War Badge: *both badges shown are good quality fakes, intended to deceive. That on the left is based on a Juncker original and is cast in a tombak-like alloy, while the badge on the right is die-struck white metal.*

Plate 20 *Reverses of items shown in* **Plate 19**. *The fake on the left has a smooth, hollow finish with the hinge forming an integral part of the badge casting. The copy on the right is also hollow, but with a mirror image of the obverse design. Its semi-broad, semi-thick pin is characteristic of fakes produced by the firm of Rudolf Souval, Vienna.*

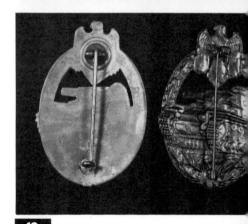

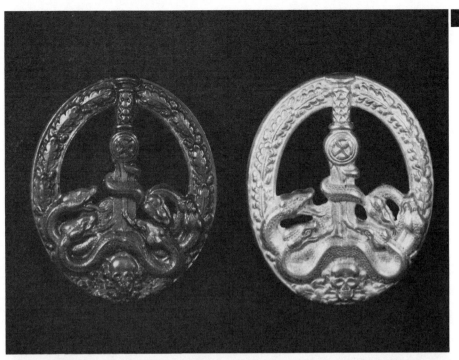

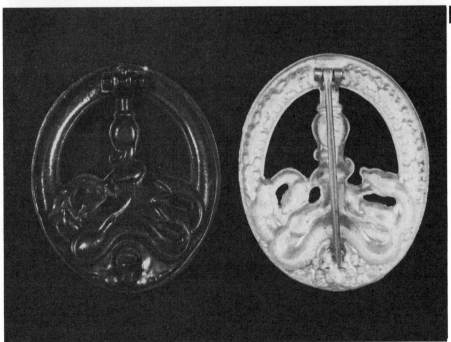

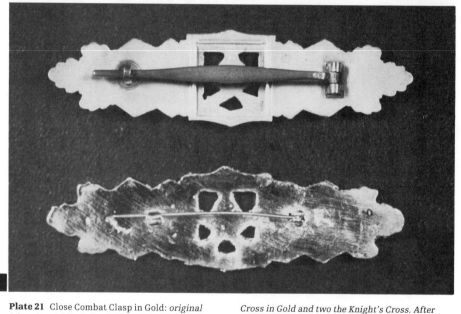

Plate 21 Close Combat Clasp in Gold: *original (above) and fake (below)*. The original is crisply die-stamped zinc with a matt gilt wash. Details are well-defined in high relief. The fake is of the film prop type, crudely cast in a brittle alloy with a glittery gilt plating. Definition is poor. The Close Combat Clasp in Gold was regarded as the senior infantry war badge, recognising participation in 50 days hand-to-hand fighting, and so it was never the subject of slipshod workmanship, particularly since Hitler reserved the right to hand it over personally. Only 400 were ever bestowed, the first 14 being awarded on 28 August 1944, to army and Waffen-SS officers, all of whom held the German Cross in Gold and two the Knight's Cross. After hearing the stories of their frontline experiences, Hitler issued a general order three days later dictating that all future winners of the Close Combat Clasp in Gold should also be regarded as having proved themselves worthy of the German Cross in Gold, if they did not already possess it.

Plate 22 *Reverse of items shown in* **Plate 21**. *The original (above) features a wide tapering pin bar and a square central recess which held a back-plate, now detached. The fake (below) has a very feeble needle pin and rough finish, with no recess.*

26

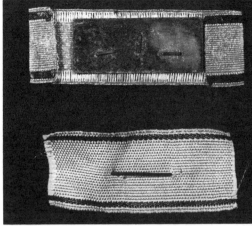

Plate 23 Tank Destruction Badge: *original (above)
and reproduction (below)*. On the original, the tank
is hollow die-stamped tombak with an oxidised
silver plating and has a short gun barrel. Note also
the thick black stripes along the edges of the heavy
aluminium thread base cloth. The tank on the
reproduction is solid and cast in a heavy grey alloy.
Its gun barrel is noticeably thinner and longer than
that on the original. The base cloth features
aluminium threads sparsely interwoven with

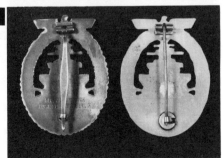

cotton, and the edge stripes are too thin. A similar
fake of the Aircraft Destruction Badge (instituted
in 1945 but never manufactured during the war),
which replaces the tank with an aeroplane, is
widely available.

Plate 24 Reverses of items shown in **Plate 23**. The
original (above) has a zinc back-plate through
which the three retaining prongs on the rear of the
tank have been pushed and bent over. The
reproduction (below) has the tank attached to the
base cloth by means of a needle pin.

Plate 25 High Seas Fleet War Badge: *original (left)
and fake (right)*. The original is convex die-stamped
brass with a heavy gilt and silver plating, typical
of materials used in the production of badges
before the end of 1942. Detail is superbly defined.
The fake in this case is one of the highest standard,
struck from an original die by the firm of Rudolf
Souval, Vienna, and made to deceive. It is also
convex, but is manufactured from a curious alloy
of aluminium and zinc which was never used in the
wartime production of this badge. Post-1942
originals were in basic zinc or kriegsmetall only,
without the aluminium content. The fake is gilded
and silvered in the correct manner, and finished off
with a protective lacquer. A very convincing piece.

Plate 26 Reverses of items shown in **Plate 25**. The
original (left) is concave and has a heavy pin bar. It
bears the marking 'Fec. Adolf Bock. Ausf. Schwerin
Berlin', ie 'Designed by Adolf Bock. Manufactured
by C. Schwerin & Sohn, Berlin'. The fake (right) is
unmarked and has a standard needle pin, which
was also used on originals. However, it is
flat-backed (the High Seas Fleet War Badge reverse
should always be concave) and the retaining clip is
typical of Souval reproductions.

27

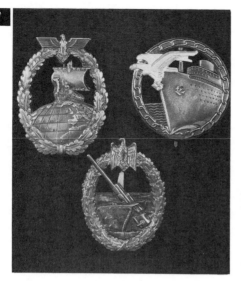

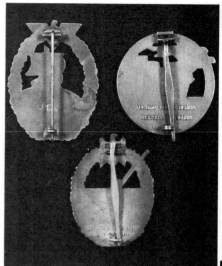

Plate 27 *Three genuine naval war badges, which illustrate the variety of materials used in the production of originals. The Auxiliary Cruiser War Badge by Orth (top left) is gilded and silvered zinc The Schwerin-made Blockade Runners Badge (top right) is lacquered zinc with frosted silver highlights. The Coastal Artillery War Badge by Juncker (below) is gilded and silver plated tombak. All are superbly detailed in high relief.*

Plate 28 *Reverses of items shown in* **Plate 27.** *Note smooth finish, crisp outlines, correct pin assemblies and makers' marks.*

Plate 29 U-Boat Combat Clasp: *original (above) and reproduction (below). The original is cast zinc with a copper plating and olive-bronze top wash. As this award was instituted in 1944, all originals were made from zinc only, not brass or tombak as were many earlier examples of the other naval war badges. The reproduction (below) is cast in a glittery, brittle, white metal alloy.*

Plate 30 *Reverses of items shown in* **Plate 29.** *The original (above) has a broad, fluted, tapering pin bar with the hinge cast into the badge, and the retaining clip soldered into a hole in the rear. It bears the marking 'Entwurf Peekhaus. Ausf. Schwerin Berlin 68', ie 'Designed by Ernst Wilhelm Peekhaus. Manufactured by C. Schwerin & Sohn, Berlin'. Schwerin was the sole maker of this rare award, so all originals should be identical to this one. The reproduction (below) displays a thin needle pin and rough finish. It also features the Schwerin markings, an unusual refinement for this type of fake.*

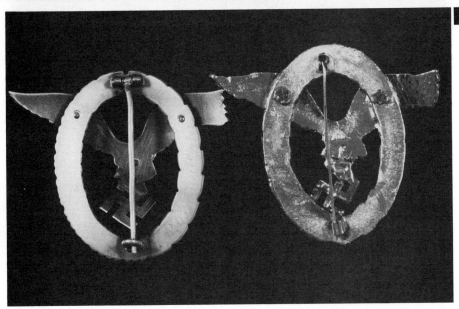

Plate 31 Pilot's Badge: *original (left) and fake (right). The original is a heavy quality convex piece die-struck from German silver, indicative of 1937-42 period manufacture. Details are well-defined in high relief and the eagle is oxidised to give a gunmetal blue finish. The fake is crudely cast in a cheap white alloy.*

Plate 32 *Reverses of items shown in* **Plate 31.** *The original (left) has the eagle affixed by two solid domed German silver rivets and the needle pin is thick and blunt-ended with a barrel hinge. This particular badge is maker marked 'OM' and has the recipient's name 'Wolfgang Hübner' scratched in Sütterlin script on the rear of the wreath. The fake (right) has the usual thin needle pin and rough soldering to retain the rivets in place. It bears the mark 'SOG' within a triangle.*

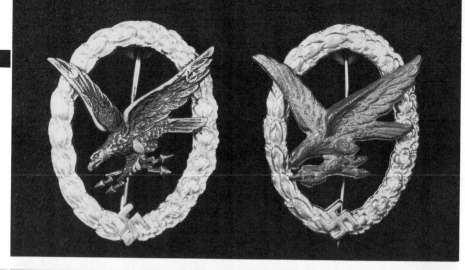

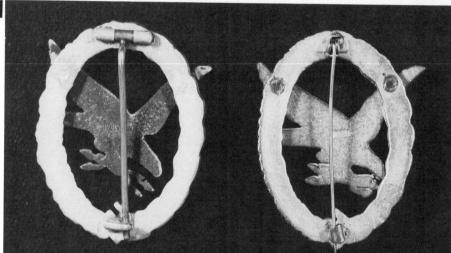

Plate 33 Radio Operator's/Air Gunner's Badge: original (left) and reproduction (right). The original is a lightweight striking in aluminium, which dates the piece to 1936-37. The wreath is polished and the eagle oxidised to give a dark grey appearance. Detail is excellent. Note in particular the clearly defined feathers and lightning bolts. The reproduction is a casting of fairly good quality, with heavy white alloy wreath and grey alloy eagle. Detail is not so crisp as on the original and the lightning bolts are squashed together.

Plate 34 Reverses of items shown in **Plate 33.** The original (left) has the eagle affixed by two solid aluminium rivets and the needle pin is again thick and blunt-ended with a barrel hinge. The fake (right) has quite passable solid grey alloy rivets,

but the finish is rough and the instant give-away is the thin needle pin, with crude hinge and unstable clip. It is interesting that both badges bear the maker's mark 'JMME'.

Plate 35 Paratrooper's Badge: original (above) and two fakes (lower left and right). The original is a late war example cast in dull zinc. The wreath has been left its natural grey colour while the eagle has been treated with a gilt wash, most of which has worn off. The fake at lower left is a recent copy of high quality, cast in a shiny zinc-based alloy with the eagle heavily gold plated. The fake at lower right is of the film prop type, crudely cast in brittle white metal and ready for painting.

30

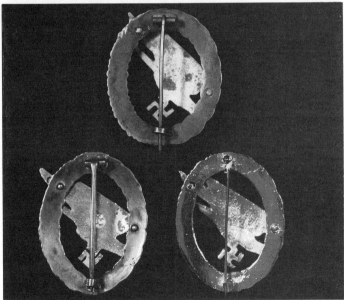

Plate 36 *Reverses of items shown in* **Plate 35.** *The original (above) is unmarked and has the eagle attached by means of two flat zinc rivets. The pin is of the standard needle type. The fake at lower left is very convincing, with proud domed rivets. Its semi-broad pin is a sure sign of reproduction, however, and the maker's mark 'SBW' within a clover leaf is an inaccurate rendition of the original clover-leafed 'BSW' logo of Gebrüder Schneider, Wien. Nevertheless, this fake might be accepted as original if offered for sale alongside the copy at lower right. The latter is crude in the extreme, with rough finishing and the usual unstable needle pin.*

Plate 37 Operational Flying Clasps: *original (top) and two reproductions (centre and bottom).* The late war original is the silver clasp for short-range night fighters and is in die-struck zinc with silver painted oakleaves and swastika and black painted laurel wreath. The winged arrow is a separate attachment in black painted brass. While the materials used are rather basic due to the period of manufacture, detail is very clearly defined and the edges of the badge are smooth. The reproduction at centre is of the bronze clasp for short-range day fighters and is cast in brass with a separate silver plated winged arrow. Detail is blurred in places and the edges rough but, otherwise, this is a fairly convincing article and has been made to pass as the real thing. The fake at bottom is a crude ˋ one-piece copy of the bronze clasp for long-range day fighters, cast in a tombak-based alloy. Note that the winged arrow is far too thick and off-centre.

Plate 38 *Reverses of items shown in* **Plate 37.** The original (top) has a smooth finish and a wide pin bar and the winged arrow is attached by a prong passed through the centre of the badge and then bent over. The reproduction at centre has a rough, pock-marked finish to the rear and close examination reveals that the 'rivet' on the rear is an artificial one forming an integral part of the casting of the badge. The silver plated winged arrow has, in fact, been soldered, not rivetted, into place. The pin is missing from this example, but it appears to have been of the semi-broad type. The fake at bottom has all the hallmarks of a crude film prop, with a thin needle pin which was never used on original Operational Flying Clasps. Once again, the central 'rivet' is false and forms an integral part of the casting.

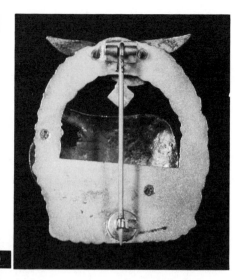

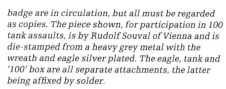

badge are in circulation, but all must be regarded as copies. The piece shown, for participation in 100 tank assaults, is by Rudolf Souval of Vienna and is die-stamped from a heavy grey metal with the wreath and eagle silver plated. The eagle, tank and '100' box are all separate attachments, the latter being affixed by solder.

Plate 40 *Reverse of item shown in* **Plate 39.** *Quality is good, with a smooth finish and sturdy rivets securing the eagle and tank. The pin and hinge are of the standard needle type, but the retaining clip is typically postwar Souval. The badge is maker stamped 'L 43', a mark not known to have been used during the Third Reich. ('43', ie without the 'L', appeared on original awards produced by Julius Bauer & Söhne, Zella-Mehlis.)*

Plate 41 *Semi-broad, semi-thick pin used on fake badges produced by the firm of Rudolf Souval, Vienna. This type of pin never featured on originals.*

Plate 39 Luftwaffe Tank Battle Badge: *fake. The Luftwaffe Tank Battle Badge was instituted in November 1944, but failed to reach production before the end of the war. Many examples of this*

Plate 42 *Fake retaining clip by Souval. This clip is simply a circular piece of sheet metal with a central strip cut out and bent over to retain the pin. Again, this type of clip was never used on originals.*

42

where two or more parts were involved these were rivetted or soldered together. Some chosen and exceptionally rare examples were elevated for particularly distinguished recipients by being encrusted with diamonds and these were made with hallmarked silver as the base metal. Each war badge was constructed with a hinge, pin and clip on its reverse for securing to the tunic. These could be of two main types: a standard needle pin most often employed on army and Luftwaffe badges; and a broad, thicker tapering version which usually featured on naval examples and which was always used on the elongated clasps. Either pattern could be affixed vertically or horizontally to the badge. Naval specimens frequently included a top hook in addition to any horizontal pin assembly, so that the badge could be kept completely flush with the tunic pocket while working in the close confines of a ship.

As with other German decorations, the manufacturers of war badges often made their company marks on them. There were well over 100 authorised makers and their trademarks varied enormously, from initials to complete addresses and from artistic monograms to simple code numbers. Moreover, these marks could be stamped or embossed. Makers' marks are no real guide when trying to determine authenticity as many genuine badges were unmarked, while fakes can easily be stamped accordingly. In particular, the firm of Rudolf Souval, Vienna, which still produces almost as many Nazi awards as it did during the Third Reich, uses the codes 'L43', L/58' or the letters 'R.S.' on its fakes.

There was always some very slight degree of diversity in detailing and finish among original pieces due to the large number of manufacturers. However, quality and overall appearance were kept consistently high right up until the end of the war. Collectors should beware of any badges exhibiting poor or blurred detailing, crude soldering techniques or construction from soft lead-based or brittle glittery alloys. Component parts joined by glue are also signs to be cautious of, as are unsubstantial pin assemblies. Some of the best fakes currently on the market belong to a range of 'variant' naval war badges, allegedly produced along the French coast during the war for purchase by locally-garrisoned German sailors. They were, in fact, created near Paris in the 1970s, being die-struck from brass then heavily plated. Each has a semi-hollow reverse and differs considerably in design from its original counterpart.

Plates 13 to **40** illustrate and comment upon a wide selection of original and fake war badges, and should provide the reader with sufficient comparative material to enable him to identify not only copies from originals, but also one type of reproduction from another and one genuine maker's variant from another. **Plates 41** and **42** show the typical fake Souval-made semi-broad pin and clip, while **Figs 2** and **3** contrast the various pin assemblies which may be found on genuine war badges with those characteristic of fakes.

THE WOUND BADGE

The construction of original 1939 wound badges varied according to the class of the award. The Wound Badge in Black was initially stamped from sheet brass, painted matt or semi-matt black, with a hollow reverse and a standard needle pin. From 1942 onwards, steel replaced brass in its manufacture and as the war dragged on so the quality of the steel declined. Consequently, the latest badges were very prone to rust. The Wound Badge in Silver was produced first from silver plated brass, then, after 1942, from white-washed zinc. It had a solid reverse with either a needle pin or a broad flat pin bar. By 1945, large numbers of hollow (ie Black grade) badges were being painted silver and issued as the higher class. Early examples of the Wound Badge in Gold were produced from gold plated brass and those made after 1942 were gilt-washed zinc. Again solid backed, the Wound Badge in Gold had a wide flat pin bar on the reverse.

At least 24 firms were authorised to make the 1939 wound badge, so slight variations

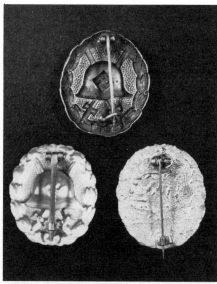

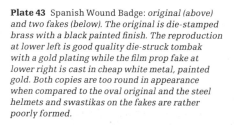

Plate 43 Spanish Wound Badge: *original (above) and two fakes (below). The original is die-stamped brass with a black painted finish. The reproduction at lower left is good quality die-struck tombak with a gold plating while the film prop fake at lower right is cast in cheap white metal, painted gold. Both copies are too round in appearance when compared to the oval original and the steel helmets and swastikas on the fakes are rather poorly formed.*

Plate 44 *Reverses of items shown in **Plate 43.** The original (above) has the hollow reverse and standard needle pin characteristic of all genuine examples of this award. The reproduction at lower left has poor definition to the reverse detailing and a spurious semi-broad pin. The fake at lower right has a solid, rough reverse and poor quality needle pin.*

Plate 45 Wound Badge of 20 July 1944: *fake, roughly cast in white metal. All originals of this exceptionally rare decoration were die-struck in hallmarked silver.*

46

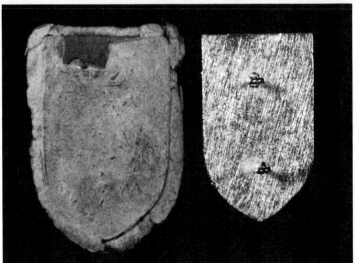

47

Plate 46 Cholm Shield: *original (left) and fake (right)*. The original is cast in heavy zinc and is backed by field grey cloth. The film prop copy is cast in a glittery white alloy and is noticeably smaller than the original.

Plate 47 *Reverses of items shown in* **Plate 46.** The original hollow shield (left) has four single prongs which have been pushed through the field grey backing cloth and secured in place by being bent over a substantial zinc back-plate. This back-plate, in turn, has been backed with rough brown paper glued into place. The fake (right) is solid, with a rough reverse. It features two lugs intended to accommodate a split pin of the sort normally encountered on British cap badges! Such is its crudity that it is difficult to imagine how this fake could ever be accepted as a genuine piece. Indeed, its use as a film prop would be extremely limited unless the reverse lugs were removed, for they protrude so much as to make wear on the left arm in the proper fashion exceedingly uncomfortable. It is more than likely that this item was produced to be permanently mounted on a 'curiosity board' displaying fake Nazi regalia of the lowest type.

in design of originals did occur, particularly in the sword hilts and the ribbon bow at the base of the wreath. Manufacturers' code numbers were frequently stamped on the reverse face or on the pin bar. Because of the large number of originals available, the 1939 wound badge has not been reproduced on the same scale or with the same care as war badges. Fakes of the Black badge tend to be stamped from brass in the correct manner, but lack detail. Their paintwork is poor and often too glossy in finish. Copies of the Silver and Gold grades are usually cast in rough quality lead-based alloys, with typically thin and unstable pin assemblies and poor soldering of fitments.

The fakers have, however, devoted more attention to the two rarer variant styles of Nazi wound badge, ie the so-called 'Spanish Wound Badge' instituted for award to Germans wounded in the Spanish Civil War of 1936-39, and the Wound Badge of 20 July 1944, presented to the few staff officers and HQ aides who sustained injury during the famous 'bomb plot' attempt on Hitler's life. All three grades of the original Spanish Wound Badge were hollow-backed die-struck plated or painted brass, with needle pins. Reproductions in hollow stamped tombak and solid cast white metal alloy, as illustrated in **Plates 43** and **44**, circulate widely. Genuine examples of the Wound Badge of 20 July 1944, which are exceedingly rare, were all die-struck in solid hallmarked silver, plated accordingly, by the firm of C. E. Juncker, Berlin. **Plate 45** shows a typical fake, cast in brittle white metal with a thin needle pin.

THE CAMPAIGN SHIELD

All of the first five 'official' campaign shields instituted during the Third Reich were hollow-backed, convex and cast or die-stamped from sheet metal in high relief detail. The first one to appear, the Narviks-child, was initially in silver or gold plated brass, then painted zinc. The Cholmschild was produced from silver painted steel or zinc while the Krimschild was in steel or zinc with an olive bronze wash. The Demjanskschild was manufactured in silver-washed zinc then plain grey zinc, and the Kubanschild in bronzed steel or zinc.

These five shields were issued with backings of woollen cloth appropriate in colour to the tunics to which they were stitched. The reverse of each shield had prongs or edge tabs, generally four in number, which were pushed through the cloth and were then secured in place by being bent over a heavy sheet steel or zinc back-plate. Early shields had this plate, in its turn, backed by cloth. Mid-war pieces had paper coverings over the plate and later examples were issued with uncovered back-plates.

Modern reproductions of the Narvik, Cholm, Krim, Demjansk and Kuban Shields come in three main forms: solid cast, hollow cast, and die-struck. The solid cast examples are usually slightly smaller than their original counterparts and are fairly crude with poor detailing and a rough reverse featuring two lugs intended to accommodate a split pin (see **Plates 46** and **47**). The hollow cast type, produced in Austria using a heavy grey alloy, is more presentable but again lacks the finer detailing of original pieces and often displays small surface stipples or pock marks on the obverse. The prongs on the reverse are poorly soldered on. The latest die-struck fakes are very convincing indeed and would fool many collectors (see **Plates 48** and **49**). They have been produced in brass, steel, aluminium and tombak with superbly defined features. However, they tend to be flat and the four prongs on the reverse are normally doubled over prior to soldering, giving the effect of eight prongs rather than four. The backing cloth is invariably felt, easily teased apart, and the back-plates are roughly cut out from thin polished tin sheeting. Copies of the Krim and Kuban Shields in this series have the appearance of light gold rather than dark bronze.

The sixth and final officially instituted and bestowed shield, the Lapplandschild, was

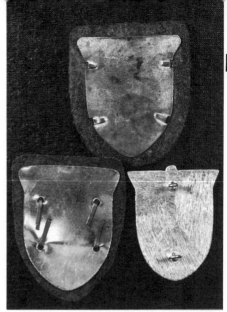

Plate 48 Kuban Shield: *original (above) and two reproductions (below left and right). The convex original is hollow die-stamped zinc sheeting with an olive bronze wash. Detail is in high relief and the shield is backed with a heavy field grey cloth. The flatter copy at lower left is one of excellent quality and would undoubtedly fool many collectors. It is in hollow die-stamped tombak-based alloy, with a golden bronze plating and a surface lacquer. Features are superbly defined, although the wings of the eagle are rather too wide and the oakleaf wreath around the swastika is too large. This piece is backed with bottle-green felt. The reproduction at lower right is a solid, poorly cast copy from the same series as the fake Cholm Shield shown in* **Plates 46** *and* **47.**

Plate 49 *Reverses of items shown in* **Plate 48.** *The original (above) has four edge tabs secured in place by a heavy, convex zinc back-plate. The copy at lower left features a roughly cut back-plate in a thin, polished tin sheeting. The prongs are in fact 'double prongs', ie there are eight prongs, not four. Such an arrangement was not known on originals. The fake at lower right has two lugs to hold a split pin in place, again never seen on originals.*

Plate 50 Lorient Shield: *reproduction. Many collectors doubt the very existence of this award, as no photographs of it being worn during the war are known. However, it is alleged to have been roughly produced by the besieged recipients themselves in steel, brass, copper, tin, chrome, aluminium and any other material available to them. The fake shown, cast in solid brass, was purchased directly from the Gloucester maker. Other copies in thin tin sheeting with prongs on the reverse circulate widely.*

Plate 51 Driver's Badge: *originals (above left and right) and copy (below). The original at top left is hollow die-stamped tombak with a bronze plating and is backed with field grey cloth. The original at top right is hollow die-stamped zinc with a silver-white wash. Its cloth backing is in Luftwaffe blue. The fake is solid cast in white metal alloy and is unbacked.*

Plate 52 *Reverse of items shown in* **Plate 51.** *The original at top left features a tombak back-plate and two edge tabs while that at top right has a zinc back-plate and two prongs. The fake (below) has two lugs for a split pin.*

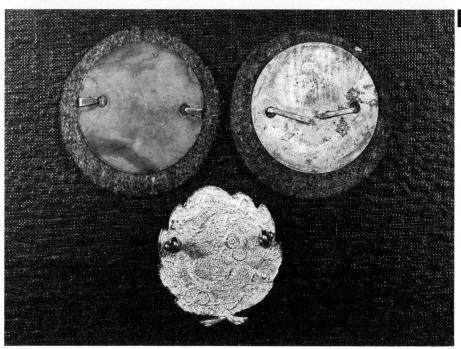

'home-made' by German prisoners-of-war during May-July 1945, and differed significantly from its predecessors. The original Lapplandschild had countless variants, all of which were very crudely cast, stamped, or even cut out from aluminium, tin or zinc. It did not have a backing cloth or plate but rather three or four holes drilled around the edges, by means of which it was stitched to the tunic. Modern copies are of die-stamped brass with the usual reverse prongs or edge tabs and are far superior in quality and detail to the real thing.

Like the Lapplandschild, the three unofficially instituted shields were very crudely made. The Lorientschild, independently approved by General der Artillerie Fahrmbacher at the end of 1944, was allegedly stamped out in the besieged U-boat base from any available materials including steel, brass, copper, tin and aluminium. No wartime photograph of this award being worn has ever come to light, and as time passes its very existence becomes more doubtful. Admiral Henneke, the Naval commander at Lorient, is on record as stating that he never saw any German servicemen in the area sporting such a shield. It is now regarded by some as a postwar fantasy piece, so great caution must be exercised if one is offered for sale. The example illustrated in **Plate 50** is a known reproduction.

The Duenkirchenschild was created by Admiral Frisius, the Channel Coast commander, for the 14,000 defenders of Dunkirk which, like Lorient, remained in German hands until the armistice. In this case, however, the shield was undoubtedly produced during the war, being roughly stamped from sheet copper with edge holes. The few originals surviving measure only 32mm × 40mm, giving rise to the theory that they were meant to be worn on the field cap or shoulder strap as a unit 'tradition badge' rather than on the left sleeve in the usual manner. No fakes of the Duenkirchenschild have come to light.

The history of the Memelschild is shrouded with obscurity. Only a few examples are said to have been produced during the winter of 1944-45 when Memel was under siege by the Russians, and even they may never have been issued. The senior German officer at Memel, Generalleutnant Dr Karl Mauss, denied all knowledge of the shield after the war. It has not been faked.

Two projected campaign shields were instituted and designed but were definitely never manufactured for award. Sketches for the first, the Warschauschild, were drawn up at the end of 1944 but the dies were subsequently destroyed in an air raid and no shields were ever produced. Modern copies of the Warschauschild are roughly cast in solid tombak with no prongs on the reverse. A few have edge holes. They are alleged to have been cast from an original plaster mould which survived the war, although this is very doubtful. A design for the Balkanschild was also approved, early in 1945, but due to the late stage of the war it was never produced. Copies circulate stamped from aluminium alloy with prongs on the reverse and feature a pigeon-like eagle and disjointed swastika.

Any examples of the so-called 'Arnheimschild', 'Stalingradschild', 'Afrikaschild' and 'Atlantikschild' which may be encountered should be avoided at all costs. These postwar fantasies were created and manufactured in England in 1979! Complete with backing cloth and plate, each shield was stamped from rusted steel, giving it a worn appearance even when new.

The Driver's Badge of Merit was produced in exactly the same way as the 'official' campaign shields and it, too, has been faked, using identical methods. **Plates 51** and **52** illustrate original variants and a typical copy.

THE CAMPAIGN CUFF TITLE

All four campaign cuff titles instituted during the Third Reich have been faked (see **Plates 53** to **56**).

The original Kreta cuff title measured 33mm in width and was of a sturdy white or cream-coloured linen cloth with the word

'Kreta' and two stylised acanthus leaf scrolls tightly machine-embroidered in yellow cotton thread. The borders, also of yellow cotton, were stitched separately on to the base cloth. Paper-backed reproductions in gold wire and thick white felt, often purporting to be so-called 'officer issue', circulate widely. Other fakes have been produced from the proper materials but are flimsy to the touch and feature a poor quality embroidery with thin lettering.

The Afrika cuff title, having a soft light-brown base cloth, almost velvety in texture, and silver-grey cotton thread embroidery, was constructed in exactly the same way as the Kreta title. Reproductions are again of two main types, the first with silver wire thread on a brown felt base and the second having crude white cotton embroidery on a rough brown linen base. The palm trees in particular are badly formed on these fakes.

The Metz 1944 cuff title was originally to take the form of a black rayon band with silver wire edging and the legend 'Metz 1944' embroidered in silver-grey thread. However, it was never officially placed into production, although a few crude examples are believed to have been manufactured at the frontline. Postwar fakes have been mass-produced in various styles, both embroidered and woven, and are generally of excellent quality.

The Kurland cuff title was instituted on 12 March 1945, as Hitler's last award to the German forces in World War 2. It was to have been about 33mm wide, of aluminium thread, with the legend and upper and lower borders embroidered in black cotton. However, domestic production difficulties and the fact that the recipients were encircled by the Russians led to all the wartime titles being produced inside the Courland Pocket by the troops themselves. The initial intention to have aluminium thread bands had to be shelved in favour of a readily available silvery-grey-white linen cloth base and the planned embroidery was replaced by a rough weave. The resultant titles were 40mm rather than 33mm wide, but were cut short to conserve material and so did not extend around the entire circumference of the cuff. Fakes of the Kurland title abound, some in felt and others in silver wire. Most are embroidered rather than woven and all are full-length and far superior in quality to the real thing.

MISCELLANEOUS MILITARY MEDALS

In addition to the badges, shields, cuff titles and other unorthodox decorations previously described, all of the more conventional military campaign, occupation and service medals awarded during the Third Reich have been faked. These can be covered 'en masse', since all fake medals of whatever design tend to feature the same characteristics.

Original Nazi medals were always die-struck, with smooth edges, good high relief detailing and thick suspension rings. The earliest examples, including the 'Flower Wars' and Wehrmacht Long Service Medals, were produced in brass, tombakbronze, aluminium and German silver and were heavily plated. From 1942, these materials were replaced by gold or silver-washed zinc. Thus, any original late war medal, such as the Blue Division Medal of 1944, would never be in brass or one of the earlier materials.

Reproduction medals tend to be of two types: cast and die-struck. The cast variety is by far the most common and while a few of these fakes are in brass or tombak, the majority are cast in a soft lead-based alloy which bends under slight pressure (see **Plate 57**), or in a glittery brittle alloy which snaps when pressurised. Many cast fakes have fairly good detailing, but all are readily identifiable as reproductions by the fact that they have a casting seam around the rim, as illustrated in **Plate 58**. Pock marks are also occasionally evident on cast copies. Examples of the die-struck type of reproduction are, fortunately, few and far between. They do not feature a casting seam and are normally stamped from original dies. However, most are struck in the wrong metals, lack the high relief quality in their detailing, and have suspension rings of a very thin wire.

41

Plate 53 Kreta, Afrika and Kurland Cuff Titles: *all originals. The Kreta title features cotton embroidery on a linen base while the Afrika title is cotton on a soft, velvet-like base cloth. The Kurland title is cotton roughly woven into a linen base.*

Plate 54 *Reverses of items shown in* **Plate 53**.

Plate 55 Metz 1944 and Grossdeutschland Cuff Titles: *both reproductions. The Metz 1944 title is BEVo woven and of excellent quality. Other fine copies of this award have been produced in neat embroidery. A photograph dating from March 1945 shows a Metz 1944 title being worn, but there is no doubt that the few originals manufactured during the war were not professionally done but were roughly custom-made at the front-line by the troops themselves. The Grossdeutschland fake is embroidered in grey cotton on a heavy bottle-green felt base almost 3mm thick, and is similar in style to reproductions of the Kreta, Afrika and Kurland titles. Felt was never used on originals. Moreover, the actual form of the title, ie Sütterlin script on green, is a postwar fantasy. The four original variants of the title were: BEVo woven Gothic lettering on green (September 1939); BEVo woven Gothic lettering on black (May 1940); embroidered Sütterlin script on black (October 1940); and embroidered Latin lettering on black (November 1944).*

Plate 56 *Reverses of items shown in* **Plate 55**. *The Metz 1944 title is one of a series of identically made fakes encompassing most of the Waffen-SS divisional and regimental cuff titles. All reproductions in this series have a typically white reverse with clearly defined tightly-woven black lettering and no loose threads. The fake Grossdeutschland title (below) has a heavy fibre-paper backing glued into place to prevent the felt from fraying.*

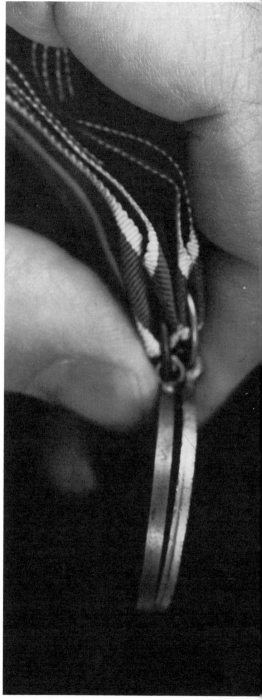

Plate 57 Memel Medal: *original (left) and reproduction (right). The original is die-struck tombak with a bronze plating. Detail is crisp and in high relief. The copy is cast in lead with a bronze wash and can be bent easily by mere finger pressure. Detail is less distinct. Note also that the ribbon ring retaining eye at the top of the medal is too wide.*

Plate 58 *Rims of items shown in **Plate 57**. The rim of the die-struck original (left) is smooth, like that of a coin. The rim of the fake (right) clearly shows the casting seam. Any alleged Nazi medal, of whatever type, which bears such a seam must be considered a reproduction.*

The entire series of civil and NSDAP decorations has been faked. A few reproductions, such as that illustrated in **Plates 59** and **60**, are made to deceive collectors but most copies, like the one shown in **Plate 61**, are fairly obvious as such by virtue of their crude appearance. Metal used is generally too soft or brittle, or of the wrong type; enamel is sparingly applied and easily chipped; details are blurred; swastikas are ungeometric; suspension rings are too thin and wire-like; casting edge seams or pock marks are visible, and so on. Needless to say, only one or two of these indicators may be encountered on a single fake, but they give a general idea of what to look for. It should be borne in mind that all official decorations, even at the end of the war, were manufactured under strictly-controlled conditions. The standard of metals used may have declined, but a fine quality of finish was always maintained (see **Plate 62**). When examining a prospective purchase, remember that sloppy workmanship was never tolerated in the Third Reich!

It is worth exploding the myth that all NSDAP awards and badges need to be RZM marked to be genuine. RZM marking did not get into full swing until 1935, so items produced before that date either bore makers' marks or none at all (see **Plates 63 to 66**). Most NSDAP decorations, such as the German Order, Blood Order and Golden Party Badge, were never RZM marked in any case, even after 1935, as the Party Headquarters in Munich invariably placed its own contracts with Deschler and other notable manufacturers rather than going through the laborious RZM system. Only if a badge was produced by a firm contracted by the RZM to make it would it be marked with the RZM symbol and the firm's RZM code number.

The more common Third Reich sports awards such as the German National Sports Badge and SA Military Sports Badge were issued in numbers so vast as to preclude the need for serious faking. Rarer items, however, like the ones illustrated in **Plates 67 to 70**, have been widely copied and even the humble Hitler Youth Proficiency Badge has been reproduced (see **Plates 71** and **72**). Fake sports badges tend to exhibit the same characteristics as fake war badges, already described, so need no further coverage here.

PRESENTATION CASES AND PACKETS

All of the protective cases and packets allocated to Third Reich awards have been reproduced. Original hinged cases for decorations such as the Iron Cross First Class were made of thin wood or thick cardboard, with a paper covering pebbled to simulate leather. The lid exterior usually bore a representation of the award contained within, or a national emblem, or the LDO logo. The inside of the lid was lined with artificial silk, padded with a cotton wool material, and the base was in velvet or flocking with a recess to accommodate the decoration. Reproduction cases are typically of plastic or thin cardboard construction and are generally too new-looking. Their exterior lid designs are frequently mis-shapen and the lid interiors are nylon-lined and padded with plastic foam sponge.

More lowly decorations such as war badges, the West Wall Medal, War Merit Medal, and Iron Cross Second Class were distributed in paper packets. Original packets were beige or blue in colour and featured the title of the decoration concerned printed in black on the front and the maker's name on the back. The paper used was thick and hard-wearing and had a flecked quality to it. Reproduction packets tend to be of thinner paper without the flecking. They are generally made in a 'blank' form, ie minus the printed title on the front, so that they can be interchanged between decorations. Once each packet has been allocated to a

Plate 59 Cross of Honour of the German Mother: original (left), original miniature (above right) and reproduction (below right). The convex original at left is die-struck tombak with a silver plating. The blue enamel portions are translucent. The miniature is similarly made with exquisite detailing. The reproduction is die-struck white metal alloy with a heavy gold plating and correctly soldered central disc. Undoubtedly it has been made to deceive, but is let down by the fact that it is too flat and slightly mis-shapen. The white enamel edges are too wide, the swastika too small and the blue enamel is opaque.

Plate 60 *Reverses of items shown in* **Plate 59**. *The inscription on the fake is less clear than that on the full-size original and even fails to reach the crisp standard of definition apparent on the miniature. The latter bears the maker's code mark 'L/11', ie Wilhelm Deumer, Lüdenscheid.*

46

Plate 61 Faithful Service Decoration: *original (above) and fake (below). The original is die-struck tombak with a gold plating and black enamel swastika while the copy is poorly cast in a glittery yellow alloy with painted swastika. Note that the reproduction has a hole drilled in its upper arm and is suspended as a neck decoration in a totally spurious manner.*

Plate 62 Luftschutz Medal: *original. This item is cast zinc. The white wash has worn off to leave an unattractive slate grey appearance, typical of late war pieces. Note, however, that despite the poor quality of the raw material used, all details are still crisply defined.*

Plate 63 Gau Munich Commemorative Badge of 9 November 1923; *original. This award was created in 1933 and presented by the Munich Gau of the NSDAP to those who had taken part in the ill-fated Munich Putsch. It never received recognition as a national award, however, and was replaced by the Blood Order in 1934. It is superbly die-stamped in high relief tombak with a bronze plating.*

Plate 64 *Reverse of item shown in* **Plate 63**. *The badge bears the full maker's name 'Deschler & Sohn, München', as this decoration was cancelled prior to 1935 when RZM code numbers were introduced. It illustrates graphically the point that not all Party awards and badges were RZM marked. Too many collectors rely on the presence of such marks when endeavouring to determine authenticity!*

Plate 65 *Badge for the SA Rally at Brunswick, 1931: originals (above left and right) and reproduction (below). This item was initially sold as a day badge to those who attended the rally but it continued to be worn by holders and in 1936 was elevated to the status of an NSDAP veteran's decoration. The original at top left is one of the early day badges, die-stamped in thin tin sheeting with a silver plating. It is very low in relief. The original at top right was produced between 1933 and 1935, since it bears no RZM mark. It is expertly struck in high relief German silver and is more oval in shape than the earlier version. The fake (below) is cast in a heavy white metal alloy.*

Plate 66 *Reverses of items shown in* **Plate 65**. *Both originals are hollow and the one at top left still bears the 1931 sale price '·35' (ie 35 Pfennigs) in indelible ink. The fake (below) displays rough craze marks caused by a poor casting technique. Its pin is of the thin needle type and is retained by a Souval-type clip.*

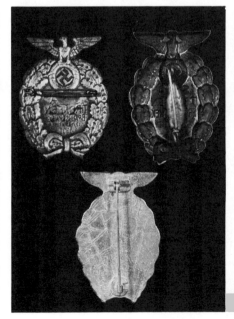

67

68

Plate 67 SA Sports Badge for War Wounded:
*original (left) and fake (right). The superbly
detailed original is heavy, die-stamped zinc with a
bronze wash. Instituted in October 1943, all
originals of this award were produced from zinc,
not tombak, brass, German silver or any of the
other earlier materials. Note the 'opfer-rune', the
ancient Nordic symbol of self-sacrifice, at the base
of the badge. The fake is cast crudely in a glittery
gold-coloured metal.*

Plate 68 *Reverse of items shown in **Plate 67**. The
original (left), with its broad pin bar, bears the
code number 'RZM M1/100' of Werner Redo,
Saarlautern, the sole manufacturer of this award.
The fake (right) is unmarked with a typically crude
pin assembly.*

49

Plate 69 Germanic Proficiency Rune: *original. This extremely rare sports badge was awarded only to Flemish, Dutch, Norwegian and Danish members of the Germanic-SS. Less than 200 were ever presented and the badge illustrated is one of only 10 originals known to exist in collections worldwide. It is convex in form and measures 46mm in diameter. The sunwheel is of cast copper plated zinc with an olive bronze wash and the siegrunes are black enamelled die-struck tombak with silver plated edges. Construction and finish are typically German and of excellent quality.*

Plate 70 *Reverse of item shown in* **Plate 69**. *The siegrunes are secured to the sunwheel by four round tombak pins bent over at the rear. The reverse is slightly 'bubbled' in appearance and*

there is no maker's mark. Collectors should avoid any examples of this award which do not conform exactly in construction to that shown, for countless copies are in circulation. Some reproductions measure 43mm in diameter, others 44mm, 49mm or 50mm. Brass and light alloys have been used in their manufacture. Some are spuriously marked 'RZM' and others 'RZM M011'. Many have the siegrunes rivetted, soldered or glued to the sunwheel.

Plate 71 Hitler Youth Proficiency Badge: *original (left) and copy (right). The original is lightweight die-struck aluminium with a copper plating and oxidised silver top wash. The reproduction is cast in a heavy white alloy.*

Plate 72 *Reverses of items shown in* **Plate 71**. *The original (left) bears the code number 'RZM M1/63' of Steinhauer & Lück, Lüdenscheid. The letter 'B' indicates the proficiency grade of the holder. There were three grades, ie 'A', 'B' and 'C'. The fake (right) is of good quality, with the correct form of pin, but is unmarked.*

Plate 73 *Ribbons: the item at top centre is the reverse of an original ribbon bar, showing the needle pin and cloth backing neatly stitched into place. All other ribbons illustrated are postwar reproductions, cut from large rolls, and show a small selection of the vast range available — everything from the humble West Wall Medal to the German Order!*

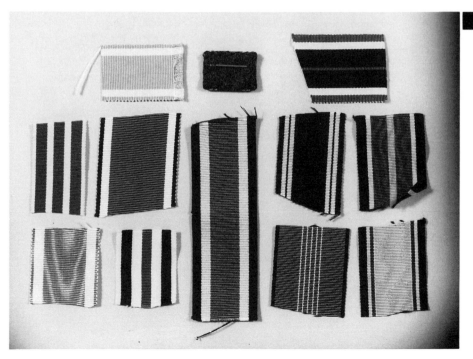

particular fake award, it is normally rubber-stamped with the title of the award in red ink. Copies of the rarer war badges such as the '50' Tank Battle Badge have recently been offered for sale in unhinged two-part boxes with a mottled paper covering in gold, yellow and white. These boxes are postwar creations and were never used as containers for war badges during the Third Reich.

RIBBONS

All types of Nazi medal ribbon have been reproduced (see **Plate 73**). Some copies are inaccurate in their colouring and proportions, while others are entirely accurate and are useful in replacing ribbons lost from original awards. Most fake ribbons, however, tend to have a hard 'feel' about them, being less silky than their Third Reich counterparts.

DE-NAZIFICATION

On 26 July 1957, the West German government passed a law on 'Titles, Orders and Medals of Honour' which made provision for the manufacture of a new range of 'de-Nazified' Third Reich decorations, for wear by veterans. The new awards held basically to their original designs but lost all vestiges of Nazism, in particular the swastika. These West German versions, which continue to be manufactured on a limited scale by Steinhauer & Lück of Lüdenscheid, feature semi-broad pins like the type used on Souval fakes and cheap, glittery, anodised 'stay-brite' alloys. They are quite inferior in quality when compared to their wartime predecessors yet, however undesirable these modern pieces might be, they are official replacements and recognised decorations and cannot be classed as reproductions *per se*. They occasionally appear on the market for sale legitimately, in their own right, but are not widely collected and fetch very low prices.

2 Dress Daggers

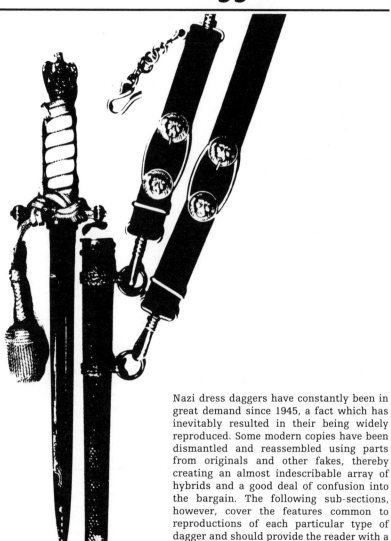

Nazi dress daggers have constantly been in great demand since 1945, a fact which has inevitably resulted in their being widely reproduced. Some modern copies have been dismantled and reassembled using parts from originals and other fakes, thereby creating an almost indescribable array of hybrids and a good deal of confusion into the bargain. The following sub-sections, however, cover the features common to reproductions of each particular type of dagger and should provide the reader with a fairly comprehensive guide on what to look for, and beware of, when examining a piece.

The army dagger of 1935 (see **Plate 74**) was ultimately produced in many variations by dozens of different firms. Early examples were manufactured with German silver-plated tombak fittings and a plated steel scabbard; later pieces featured white-washed zinc components. The handles could be regulation white, yellow or orange in colour. Some grips were solid plastic and others took the form of plastic over a wood base; a few deluxe ones were in ivory. Crossguard eagles varied slightly in design. Certain steel blades were purer and less prone to rust than others, while etched and damascus blades were available for presentation pieces. The dagger was suspended from a hanger comprising two straps, each made of aluminium braid sewn to a field grey velvet backing. Hanger buckles and fittings were normally of plated tombak or whitened zinc (gilded for generals) and a range of styles existed to cater for the individual preferences of all prospective purchasers. If desired, a 42cm aluminium portepee knot could be wrapped around the pommel, handle and crossguard when the dagger was worn. Fakes usually have one or more of the following features:

(i) Poor definition — originals always had good detailing to the eagle, oakleaves and scabbard stippling.

(ii) Brass fittings — genuine army daggers were not constructed from brass.

(iii) Grip grooves running in the wrong direction, ie from high left to low right — they should run from high right to low left.

(iv) Grips with very sharp ridges to the grooves — originals had smooth curves.

(v) RZM stamps to the blade — army blades were never RZM marked.

(vi) Rounded edges to the flats of the blade — these should be sharply defined, as in **Plate 75**.

(vii) Scabbards with separate tips — original scabbards were constructed in one piece.

(viii) Narrow brass liners soldered into the scabbard — genuine liners were in steel or zinc alloy and were rivetted into position.

A variation army dagger was considered in 1941, but never progressed beyond the prototype stage. The design for the new dagger featured a vertically-grooved white grip, a pommel bearing Wehrmacht eagles on the obverse and reverse, and a spiralling scroll to the crossguard. It has been alleged that this sidearm was intended for wear only by Field Marshals, but no supporting documentary evidence has come to light. In any case, a dagger specifically designed for such exalted ranks would no doubt have been far more ornate. Many copies of it circulate, most with the mark of 'Ernst Pack & Söhne — Siegfried Waffen — Solingen' etched on their blades. Some display odd additions to their pommel, viz two tri-angular shields each bearing a siegrune of the type encountered on the SS Death's Head Ring, and have been offered as rare items presented by Heinrich Himmler to Waffen-SS generals.

NAVY

Like the army dagger, the 1938-pattern navy dagger (see **Plate 76**) was produced in many variations. The purchaser could opt for a plain or an etched blade, and have either a hammered or an engraved scabbard. Grips might be white, yellow or orange in colour, and be of horn, ivory, solid plastic or plastic over wood. Suspension rings could be plain or of a rope design. Collectors will find that the majority of naval sidearms encountered feature an etched blade and a scabbard engraved with lightning bolts. The dagger

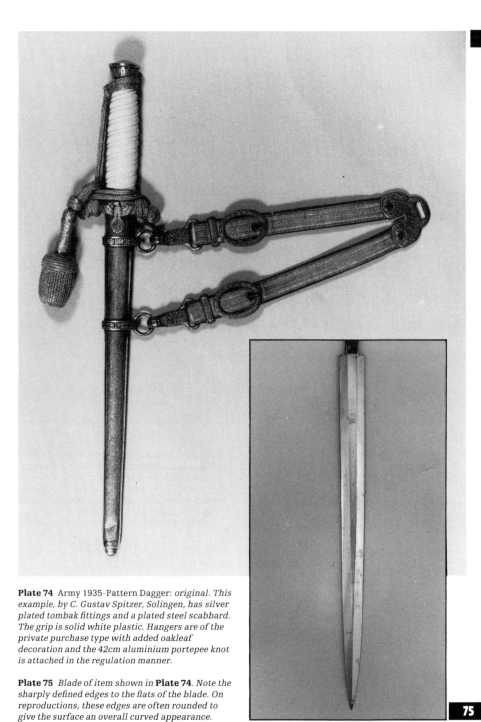

75

Plate 74 Army 1935-Pattern Dagger: *original. This example, by C. Gustav Spitzer, Solingen, has silver plated tombak fittings and a plated steel scabbard. The grip is solid white plastic. Hangers are of the private purchase type with added oakleaf decoration and the 42cm aluminium portepee knot is attached in the regulation manner.*

Plate 75 *Blade of item shown in* **Plate 74**. *Note the sharply defined edges to the flats of the blade. On reproductions, these edges are often rounded to give the surface an overall curved appearance.*

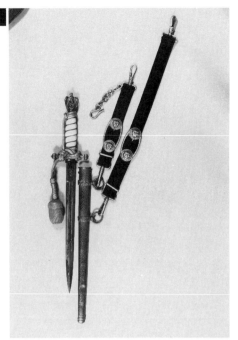

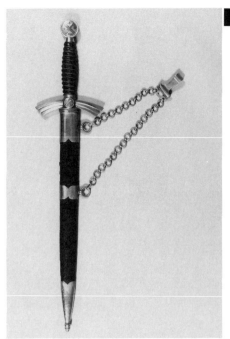

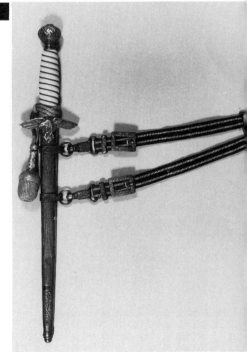

Plate 76 Navy 1938-Pattern Dagger: *original. This piece, by 'WKC' (Weyersberg, Kirschbaum & Co, Solingen), has brass fittings and scabbard with a white plastic-over-wood grip. The blade is etched with sailing ships, anchors and foliage. The hangers have gilt-washed aluminium attachments and the 42cm portepee knot is hung in the traditional so-called 'reef knot' fashion.*

Plate 77 Luftwaffe 1935-Pattern Dagger: *original. This item, by 'SMF' (Solinger Metallwarenfabrik Stöcker & Co), is an early example with silver plated tombak fittings.*

Plate 78 Luftwaffe 1937-Pattern Dagger: *original. This example is unmarked, with plain zinc components and grey steel scabbard, typical of a late war piece. The hangers are standard and the 23cm portepee knot is attached in the prescribed fashion.*

56

was suspended from two separate black straps, one longer than the other, each comprising watered silk stitched to a velvet backing. Both straps bore gilded lion-head buckles and fittings (silvered for administrative officers), and the short strap had a chain attachment which could be hooked around the pommel to keep the dagger in a vertical position. A 42cm portepee knot in gilt or silver aluminium bullion thread was normally fastened about the pommel, handle and crossguard in the traditional naval 'reef-knot' fashion.

Marine daggers are still produced in West Germany for export and wear by Federal naval personnel. The pommel eagle now holds a fouled anchor rather than a swastika in its talons, but otherwise the overall design is virtually unchanged. As a result, many modern daggers have simply had their pommels replaced by Nazi ones and have thereafter been easily passed off as wartime issues. Certain indicators do exist, however, to assist the collector in differentiating between an authentic Third Reich dagger and a touched-up postwar piece:

(i)   Loose pommels — replacements are usually slack, or off-centre, when screwed into position.

(ii) The grip — the modern grip has a very brittle plastic coating over a wood base, and a thin wire wrapping which is much finer than that used on originals.

(iii) Metals used — wartime dagger fittings and scabbards were constructed from brass, while many postwar versions are made of a heavy, yellowish tombak-based alloy. In contrast, though, original lion-head buckles and all other attachments for the hanging straps were in gilded aluminium or lightweight alloy, not brass.

(iv) Liners — several modern scabbards have plastic liners, which were never used during the Third Reich.

(v)   Incorrect etching and engraving — blades etched with a fouled anchor surmounted by a Wehrmacht eagle, or with a battleship, or with the Kiel naval monument, are postwar creations as these designs were not known prior to 1945. The same applies to scabbards engraved with battleships or sea serpents.

(vi) Incorrect makers — only 17 firms manufactured naval daggers between 1938 and 1945. These were Alcoso, Clemen & Jung, Eickhorn, Höller, Hörster, Robert Klaas, Krebs, Lauterjung, Lüneschloss, Pack, Plümacher, Puma, Paul Seilheimer, Max Weyersberg, Paul Weyersberg, WKC and Wingen. Blades bearing other makers' marks are post-1945 productions.

LUFTWAFFE

The first pattern Luftwaffe dagger of 1935 (see **Plate 77**), with its grip and scabbard wrapped in fine grain leather, was an expensive item to produce. Early examples had the metallic portions in silver plated tombak or German silver, with small connecting rings on the chain hangers, while later pieces were distinguished by their more economical aluminium fittings and larger connecting rings. Reproductions can be identified by one or more of the following features:

(i)   Deformed sunwheel swastikas on the pommel and crossguard — originals were symmetrically perfect.

(ii) Grip wire of a single double-strand — the authentic arrangement was of two double-strands lying alongside each other, or of a double-strand set between two single strands.

(iii) Ill-shaped grips.

(iv) Badly attached leather wrappings to the grip and scabbard.

(v)   Upper scabbard mounts of excessive length — the original upper mount (or 'locket') left a space of about one-and-a-half times its own length between itself and the scabbard's central mount.

(vi) Crude liners soldered into the scabbard — these should be well formed and rivetted into position.

(vii) Rounded edges to the flats of the blade — genuine blades had sharply defined edges.

(viii) RZM markings to the blade — Luftwaffe blades were never RZM stamped.

(ix)   Many reproductions bear a spurious stamped representation of the Clemen & Jung trademark, being an oval cartouche containing the words 'Clemen & Jung, Solingen' around a 'Z' within a shield. The correct Third Reich version of the mark was simply a 'Z' within a shield.

The second pattern Luftwaffe dagger introduced for officers and senior NCOs in 1937 (see **Plate 78**) was designed to be more military than political in appearance and, like its army and navy counterparts, came in many variations. Early examples bore hilt fittings of white cast aluminium while later issues had zinc-based alloy components with a dark grey finish. Some pommels had gilded swastikas while others had grey ones. Grips could be white, yellow or orange in colour and be of ivory, solid plastic or plastic over wood. The form of the crossguard eagle, particularly in the fletching of its wings, varied from maker to maker and blades might be plain or etched. The only common denominator appears to have been the scabbard, which was of grey steel in all cases. The dagger was suspended from a double-strap hanger, each strap comprising blue-grey weave with aluminium edge stripes and a velvet backing. Hanger buckles and fittings were of aluminium or zinc alloy (gilded for Generals) and again a range of styles was produced. A short 23cm aluminium bullion portepee knot could be wrapped around the ferrule, by flying personnel only, when the dagger was worn. The following characteristics are common to reproductions:

(i)   Crossguards in a heavy grey alloy — original examples, including the zinc types, were always lightweight.

(ii)   Grip wire running in the wrong direction, ie from high right to low left — it should run from high left to low right. (Note how this arrangement differs from the grooves on army and navy handles.)

(iii) Grip wire comprising a twisted double-strand — the original wire was a single-strand, thick and wavy in form.

(iv)   RZM marks to the blade — Luftwaffe blades were never RZM stamped.

(v)   Scabbards with separate tips — genuine scabbards were constructed in one piece.

(vi)   Scabbards in a grey or silver-coloured non-magnetic alloy as opposed to the steel originals.

(vii) Poor stippling behind the oakleaves on the shield at the lower end of the scabbard — this should be well defined.

(viii) Wooden or brass liners crudely fitted into the scabbard locket — genuine liners were in steel or zinc alloy and were rivetted into position.

The following sub-sections describe the salient features common to reproductions of each particular type of political and civil dagger.

SA
*SA 1933 Dagger (see **Plate 79**)*

(i)   Plastic grips — originals were in a variety of woods, especially walnut and maple, carved symmetrically, stained and varnished.

(ii)   A poorly cast eagle set too high on the grip — the top of the eagle should be level with the widest part of the grip.

(iii) Badly etched blade mottoes with ragged edges, a stippled background to the lettering, or the wording misaligned — etching should be crisp, smooth and level.

(iv)   'Germany' stamped on the blade's ricasso or tang — indicative of a postwar dagger made for export to the USA.

(v)   Sharp blade spines — genuine blades had rounded spines.

(vi)   Poorly finished scabbards with misshapen rims to the lockets (upper mounts) and chapes (lower mounts).

(vii) Cast lockets and chapes with prominent edge seams — originals were die-struck.

(viii) One-piece lockets — originals were in two sections.

(ix)   Thin scabbard liners soldered or simply pushed into place inside the locket — original liners were wide, of brass, and rivetted into position.

SA 1934 Röhm Honour Dagger
As for the SA 1933 Dagger, but with the following additional features:
(i) Poorly etched Röhm dedications — presentation etching was always of excellent quality.
(ii) Engraved Röhm dedications — originals were never engraved.
(iii) Damascus or artificial damascus Röhm blades with raised gilded lettering — never a feature of originals.
(iv) Offset dedications — the dedication should be central along the reverse spine.
(v) A maker other than Carl Eickhorn, Böker & Co, Eduard Wüsthof, Anton Wingen, Ernst Pack, Richard Herder, Gottlieb Hammesfahr, J. A. Henckels or C. G. Haenal, the only known original producers of Röhm blades.
(vi) RZM marked blades — these were not introduced until after the Röhm Honour Dagger was withdrawn from production.

SA 1935 Honour Dagger
As for the SA 1933 Dagger, but with these additional characteristics:
(i) Badly cast grip mounts in copper, brass or soft alloy with edge seams — originals were always die-struck in nickel silver or nickel plated zinc, with fine detailing to the oakleaves and acorns.
(ii) Engraved grip mounts — never encountered on originals.
(iii) Blades bearing non-Eickhorn trademarks — only Carl Eickhorn of Solingen was authorised to produce the SA 1935 Honour Dagger.
(iv) RZM marked blades — Honour Daggers were never RZM marked.
(v) Scabbards with separate lockets and chapes — genuine scabbards for this pattern were manufactured in one piece, with embossed fittings.

SA 1938 Chained Honour Dagger
As for the SA 1935 Honour Dagger, but with the following extra points:
(i) Faint background stippling to the suspension chain links — this

stippling should not be present.
(ii) Circular junction rings to the chain links — authentic examples were semi-circular.
(iii) Scabbards decorated with runic emblems, in particular sunwheel swastikas, life runes and Tyr-runes — never a feature of originals.

SA Feldherrnhalle Dagger
(i) Pommel locking nuts with twin holes — originals had cruciform slots.
(ii) Grips in soft wood — genuine examples were in hard wood.
(iii) Wooden scabbard liners — these should be of brass.
(iv) Motto etched centrally on the blade — on original examples the motto was sited much closer to the hilt than to the tip, a characteristic common to all Third Reich daggers with blade mottoes.
(v) A maker's mark other than that of Carl Eickhorn, Solingen, who was sole producer of the SA Feldherrnhalle Dagger.
(vi) Blades etched with a spurious dedication from Viktor Lutze — not known on originals.

SS
*SS 1933 Dagger (see **Plates 80** and **81***)
Reproductions have features similar to those of fakes of the SA 1933 Dagger.

SS 1934 Röhm Honour Dagger
As for the SA 1934 Röhm Honour Dagger.

SS 1934 Himmler Honour Dagger
As for the SS 1933 Dagger, but with these additional features:
(i) Poorly etched Himmler dedications, sometimes even minus the top half of the 'l' in 'Himmler' — presentation etching was always strictly controlled and of excellent quality.
(ii) Engraved Himmler dedications — originals were never engraved.
(iii) Offset dedications — the dedication should be central along the blade's reverse spine.
(iv) RZM marked blades — unknown on original Himmler Honour Daggers.
(v) Blades bearing non-Eickhorn trademarks — Carl Eickhorn of

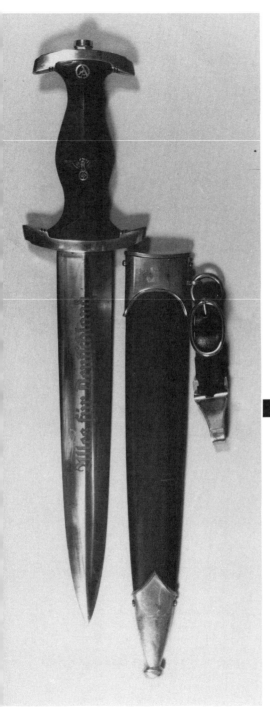

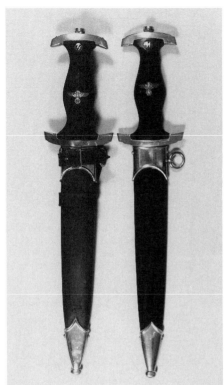

79

80

Plate 79 SA 1933-Pattern Dagger: *original. An early piece by J. A. Henckels with heavy German silver mounts and anodised scabbard.*

Plate 80 SS 1933-Pattern Dagger: *original (left) and reproduction (right). The original, by Gottlieb Hammesfahr, Solingen, is an early piece with die-struck German silver mounts and anodised scabbard. The upper scabbard mount, or locket, is made in two parts and the wide brass scabbard liners are rivetted into position. The grip is black stained wood and the high quality steel blade is finely etched with the SS motto and maker's mark. The reproduction is one of a series manufactured in Toledo, Spain. Its blade is marked 'RZM M7/36' (ie E. & F. Hörster, Solingen), but is of poor quality steel and badly rusted. The scabbard mounts are cast, with casting seams clearly visible, and the locket comprises a single piece with the scabbard liners crudely pushed into place. There are no rivets holding the liners securely in position. The grip is black plastic and the eagle is poorly finished and set too high.*

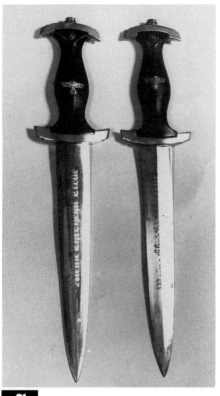

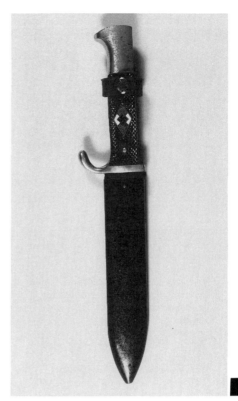

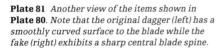

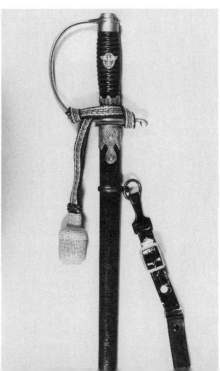

Plate 81 *Another view of the items shown in* **Plate 80***. Note that the original dagger (left) has a smoothly curved surface to the blade while the fake (right) exhibits a sharp central blade spine.*

Plate 82 Hitler Youth 1933-Pattern Hiking Knife: *original, by Carl Wüsthof.*

Plate 83 Police Senior NCO's 1936-Pattern Sword: *original, by Alcoso. Swords have not been the subject of out-and-out faking, but Police swords such as this one are often converted by having the Police eagle in the grip removed and replaced by SS runes. Sold as SS swords, they then fetch perhaps five times their original value.*

Solingen had sole manufacturing rights to the Himmler Honour Dagger. Only 200 were made and each was serially numbered.

SS 1936 Honour Dagger
As for the SA 1935 Honour Dagger, and again Eickhorn was the only producer of this pattern. None should have 'Himmler' blades. In addition, beware of exquisitely hand-made items with ivory grips allegedly presented to 'Sepp' Dietrich, Julius Schreck and other SS leaders. A few of these pieces have the would-be recipient's initials at the top of the grip, instead of the SS runes. All are postwar fantasies.

SS 1936 Chained Dagger
As for the SS 1933 Dagger, but with these extra points:
(i)   Poorly detailed or ill-fitting central scabbard mounts — authentic mounts were sharply die-struck with high relief swastikas and background stippling.
(ii)   Roughly cast chain links bearing pock marks and other flaws — originals were crisply die-stamped in nickel silver, or in nickel plated steel or zinc.
(iii)   'Gruppe' stamps to the reverse lower crossguard — the sign of a 'parts' assembly. All SS 1936 Chained Daggers had to be privately purchased from the SS Uniform Centre in Berlin, so were not issue stamped.

NSKK
NSKK 1933 Dagger
Reproductions have features similar to those of fakes of the SA 1933 Dagger.

NSKK 1936 Chained Dagger
As for the NSKK 1933 Dagger, but with the following additional indicators:
(i)   Loosely attached scabbard central mounts — genuine mounts were made to fit well with no large gaps.
(ii)   Very thin raised borders to the central mount — original lips were usually quite substantial and in any case always matched those on the corresponding locket and chape. A mis-match may mean that the piece under consideration is simply a 1933 dagger with spurious postwar chains

and accompanying central mount added.
(iii)   Poorly defined suspension chain links, cast in a soft alloy — originals were well struck in either nickel silver or nickel plated steel.
(iv)   Circular junction holes to the chain links — authentic examples were domed with a flat base.
(v)   Chain links bearing the spurious inscription 'Muster geschützt NSKK Korpsführer' ('Pattern Copyright of the NSKK Supreme Commander') — original chains were stamped 'Musterschutz NSKK Korpsführung' ('Copyright of the NSKK High Command') on the reverse of one of the two upper links only. The back of the chain's other upper link usually featured the RZM code number 'M5/8' of the sole manufacturer, Assmann.

NSKK 1938 Dagger
This variant dagger, of which only three allegedly exist, is very similar in design to the second pattern Luftwaffe dagger, but with an NSKK eagle on the crossguard. It has erroneously been called the 'High Leader's Dagger', and it has also been attributed to officers of NSKK transport regiments serving with the Luftwaffe. However, no wartime photographs of it being worn have come to light and it is probably a postwar fantasy. Any example offered should be viewed with great scepticism.

NPEA
NPEA 1935 Dagger
(i)   Plastic grips — originals were carved from a variety of woods.
(ii)   Badly etched, oversized or disjointed blade mottoes — genuine etching was always neat (smaller than that of the SA, SS and NSKK mottoes), uniform and of high quality.
(iii)   A depressed or 'scooped out' background to the blade motto, indicative of an original SA blade which has had its motto erased and replaced by that of the NPEA.
(iv)   Crossguards bearing SA Gruppe marks — again commonly encountered on so-called NPEA daggers which are, in fact, original SA daggers with re-

etched blades and other minor modifications.

(v) Blades bearing a trademark other than that of Eickhorn or Burgsmüller — further evidence of conversion, since Eickhorn was the sole manufacturer, and Burgsmüller the sole distributor, of NPEA daggers.

(vi) Blades marked 'Karl Burgsmüller, Berlin-Charlottenburg 5' — the original trademark of this firm was simply 'Karl Burgsmüller, Berlin'.

(vii) Separate scabbard tips soldered into position — yet another sign of the converted SA dagger. Original NPEA 1935 scabbards were formed in a single piece, each with an integral hollow tip.

(viii) 'Germany' stamped on the blade ricasso or tang — the sign of a postwar copy made for export to the USA.

(ix) Sharp blade spines — genuine NPEA blades had rounded spines.

(x) Scabbard liners in a thin grey alloy — originals were wide and made of brass.

(xi) Four grooves to the scabbard's frog stud — originals had only two grooves.

NPEA 1936 Chained Dagger
As for the NPEA 1935 Dagger — except points (vii) and (xi) — but with the additional feature:

(i) Aluminium suspension chains with large connecting rings in the style of later examples of the 1935 Luftwaffe Dagger — original NPEA chains were of nickel plated brass, steel or zinc, with small connecting rings.

NSFK
NSFK 1937 Dagger
(i) Roughly cast fittings — originals were devoid of flaws.

(ii) Painted swastikas to the crossguard — these should be finely executed in black enamel.

(iii) Unmarked scabbard lockets — genuine lockets bore the NSFK stamp, or the DLV stamp, or both.

(iv) Scabbard lockets with attachment screws at the lower end — originals had these screws situated at the top, immediately beneath the throat.

(v) Scabbard chapes with spherical tips —

originals were flattened to produce an oval effect.

RAD
RAD 1934 Hewer
(i) Crudely cast, chrome plated alloy hilts — originals were expertly cast in nickel silver or nickel plated steel.

(ii) Roughly etched blade mottoes, with a stippled background to the lettering — etching should be smooth and well defined.

(iii) Mottoes etched so as to read from the tip of the blade towards the ricasso — genuine RAD mottoes were etched to be read from the hilt end of the blade towards the tip (ie unlike those of the SA, SS, NSKK and NPEA).

(iv) RZM marked blades — RAD sidearms were never RZM stamped.

(v) Ill-formed designs to the locket and chape — original scabbard mounts were clearly embossed (never etched) with the looped runic pattern and RAD insignia.

(vi) Lockets and chapes in a lightweight grey alloy — originals were in nickel silver, or nickel plated steel or zinc.

RAD Leader's 1937 Hewer
(i) Hilts cast in a heavy grey alloy — originals were in either nickel plated steel or aluminium.

(ii) Points (ii) to (v) as per the RAD 1934 Hewer.

Hitler Youth
Hitler Youth 1933 Knife (see **Plate 82***)*
(i) Grip insignia glued into position — originals had the Hitler Youth diamond secured by means of two prongs which were pushed through retaining slots in the obverse grip facing and then bent over, prior to assembly of the handle.

(ii) Blades stamped with the word 'Solingen' on its own — a feature not encountered on Third Reich pieces but commonly found on modern Scout knives. Many of these modern knives are identical in pattern to the Hitler Youth 1933 knife, and easily converted by removal of the 'Fleur-de-lys' diamond from the grip and its replacement by fake Nazi grip insignia.

(iii) Post 1938 dated blades etched with the

Hitler Youth motto 'Blut and Ehre!' in imitation of Baldur von Schirach's handwriting — this motto appeared only on knives produced prior to August 1938.
(iv)	Alloy scabbards — these should be made from steel.
(v)	Scabbards having a raised lip at the throat — originals had no lip.

Hitler Youth Bayonet
A large number of bayonets are in circulation which purport to have been worn by elite Hitler Youth units such as the HJ-Streifendienst and bodyguard of the Reichs-jugendführer. They are, in fact, postwar conversions comprising the standard army dress bayonet with a copy of the Hitler Youth diamond glued into a recess in the grip. There is no photographic evidence to support the theory that such bayonets were issued, even on a limited scale, during the Third Reich.

Hitler Youth Leader's 1937 Dagger
(i)	Badly cast alloy pommels — originals were made from nickel plated steel or aluminium, with crisp high relief Hitler Youth insignia.
(ii)	Plastic grips — each genuine handle took the form of a carved wood base wrapped overall in fine silver wire.
(iii)	Blades bearing the spurious etched dedication 'Für verdienste um die Deutsche Jugend' ('For merit in the German Youth Movement') — not known on originals.
(iv)	Cheap quality scabbard coverings — genuine scabbards were finished in high grade leather.
(v)	Poorly detailed locket eagles — these should be well executed.
(vi)	Locket eagles holding swords and spanners — originals held swords and hammers.
(vii)	Locket eagles in a stationary, almost 'guardant' pose — genuine examples were depicted 'taking off' towards the viewer's right.

Police
The Waterways Police Dagger was based largely on the standard navy dagger and fakes of it parallel those of the latter, as already described.

Members of all the other Nazi civil police formations did not wear daggers, preferring instead to sport their more traditional sidearms. Junior ranks were provided with dress bayonets and many excellent copies of these edged weapons have been produced. Features to be wary of are grip insignia glued into position (they should be pinned or rivetted), and an excessive use of plating in order to conceal casting flaws or rough base metal. No piece should be RZM marked. Officers and senior NCOs carried swords on formal occasions until 1942, when their wear was forbidden by Himmler for the duration of the war (see **Plate 83**). These have not been reproduced, although some originals have been 'enhanced' by bogus etching or the application of fake SS insignia. All Nazi issue swords, particularly the Luftwaffe type illustrated in **Plate 84**, were expensive to manufacture and, consequently, none has been seriously copied since the capital costs which the faker would have to incur would be prohibitive.

Reichsbahn
Reichsbahn 1935 Dagger
Reproductions have characteristics similar to those of fakes of the army dagger.

Reichsbahn 1938 Dagger
(i)	Brass hilt fittings — never seen on authentic railway daggers. Genuine pommels, ferrules and crossguards were die-cast in aluminium or nickel plated zinc.
(ii)	Rounded edges to the flats of the blade — these should be sharply defined.
(iii)	Heavy, grey-coloured steel scabbards — originals were made from aluminium or nickel plated steel and were always lightweight.
(iv)	Loosely attached scabbard liners in wood or plastic — these should be of steel or zinc alloy and securely rivetted into position.

Postschutz
Postschutz 1939 Dagger
(i)	Soft wood handles coated with black ink which can easily be washed off — original grips were in hard wood, permanently stained black.
(ii)	Poor detailing to the grip insignia — such badges were always well formed.

(iii) Crossguards featuring painted swastikas — originals were enamelled.

(iv) Hilt and scabbard fittings roughly cast in brass with a light silver plating — genuine examples were finely executed in nickel silver, nickel plated steel or nickel plated zinc.

(v) Blades bearing a maker's mark other than that of Paul Weyersberg, Solingen — Weyersberg was the sole producer of the Postschutz dagger.

Luftschutz

Luftschutz 1936 Other Rank's Dagger
Luftschutz 1936 Officer's Dagger
Luftschutz 1938 Other Rank's Dagger
Luftschutz 1938 Officer's Dagger
As for the Postschutz 1939 Dagger, points (i), (ii) and (iv) apply in all cases.

Fire Brigade

Other Rank's Dress Axe
Fire Officer's Dagger
Both of these items were introduced prior to World War 1, and their original designs remained unchanged throughout the Nazi period. They continue to be manufactured, in identical styles, for wear by today's firemen on formal occasions. Short of presentation inscriptions, or dated trademarks, there is nothing to distinguish a Third Reich Fire Brigade sidearm from an imperial or federal one. Consequently, the question of identifying fakes, *per se*, does not really arise.

TeNo

TeNo 1938 Hewer
(i) Pitted hilts, crudely cast in chrome plated brass or alloy — originals were finely crafted from nickel silver or nickel plated steel.

(ii) Unmarked grips — each original grip facing had the Eickhorn trademark stamped on its reverse, prior to assembly.

(iii) Blades featuring a maker's mark other than that of Carl Eickhorn, Solingen — Eickhorn was the patentee of all TeNo edged weapons.

(iv) Poorly etched blade markings — authentic representations of the Eickhorn logo and TeNo eagle were well executed.

(v) RZM marked blades — TeNo blades were never RZM marked.

(vi) Thin scabbard liners soldered to the inside of the locket — genuine liners were rivetted into position.

TeNo 1938 Dagger
As for the TeNo 1938 Hewer, points (iii) to (vi) apply, but with these additional indicators:

(i) Badly formed hilt fittings in a variety of plated alloys — originals were keenly cast in aluminium, oxidised to give a tarnished appearance.

(ii) Scabbards in silver plated brass — genuine examples were in oxidised steel.

(iii) Scabbards with elongated tips — the chape should terminate in a flattened oval.

(iv) Blades bearing etched dedications from Dr Fritz Todt or SS-Gruppenführer Hans Weinreich — never featured on originals.

Note: Each original TeNo sidearm which was actually issued bore a distribution number stamped into the blade ricasso and also into the scabbard locket. Many fakes have been similarly numbered, whereas unissued examples held in storage during the war were obviously without this feature. In short, collectors should never view distribution stampings as a sure sign of authenticity.

Customs Service

Land Customs 1937 Dagger
(i) Heavy alloy or brass hilt fittings — originals were die-cast in nickel plated steel or aluminium.

(ii) Grip grooves and wire running in the wrong direction, ie from high left to low right — they should run from high right to low left.

(iii) Grip wire in the form of a twisted double strand, bordered on either side by a single strand — the original style was simply a twisted double strand.

(iv) Rounded edges to the flats of the blade — these should be sharply defined.

(v) RZM marks on the blade — Customs daggers were never RZM stamped.

(vi) Blades bearing a lightly etched version of the 'F.W. Höller, Solingen' trademark — this is the most common mark found on reproduction Customs daggers. Original Höller logos were deeply etched or stamped, with fine detailing to the thermometer.

(vii) Plastic scabbards — genuine examples were steel-based.

(viii) Cheap, synthetic coverings to the scabbard and grip — originals were wrapped in soft green leather.

(ix) Narrow brass liners soldered into the scabbard — these should be of steel or zinc alloy, rivetted into position.

Water Customs 1937 Dagger
As for the Land Customs 1937 Dagger, but with gilded metal parts and blue-coloured leather wrappings.

Diplomatic Corps and Government Administration
Diplomatic Corps 1938 Dagger
Government Administration 1939 Dagger

(i) Lightweight alloy fittings — original parts were in silver plated brass.

(ii) Unmarked fittings — each genuine component was stamped during manufacture with an identification number, positioned so as to be hidden from view when the dagger was assembled.

(iii) White plastic grips — these should be simulated mother-of-pearl over wood.

(iv) Crossguard reverses which are rough and unplated, or which feature two circular ejector pin marks — original crossguards had smooth plated reverses.

(v) Rounded edges to the flats of the blade — these should be well defined.

(vi) RZM marked blades — neither Diplomatic Corps nor Government Administration daggers were RZM marked.

(vii) Scabbards with separate tips — genuine scabbards were constructed with integral tips.

(viii) Scabbard throats soldered into place — originals were affixed by means of two screws.

Red Cross
Red Cross 1938 Hewer

(i) Poorly cast aluminium hilt fittings — originals were in nickel silver or nickel plated steel.

(ii) Wooden grips — genuine examples were in black plastic.

Red Cross 1938 Dagger

(i) Lack of detail to the crossguard cartouche — originals were crisply defined.

(ii) RZM marked blades — Red Cross sidearms were never RZM marked.

Forestry Service and Hunting Associations
A wide variety of German forestry and hunting daggers existed long before the advent of the Third Reich, and their basic designs remained unaltered throughout the Nazi period. They are still being produced today. A few modern examples, however, have incorporated spurious eagles and swastikas in an attempt to deceive collectors. Points to look out for are as follows:

(i) Gold plated tombak hilt fittings — fittings manufactured between 1933 and 1945 were in brass or aluminium.

(ii) Plastic handles — Third Reich grips were individually carved from staghorn or wood.

(iii) Plastic scabbards — these should be leather.

German Rifle Association
German Rifle Association 1939 Dagger

(i) Ill-formed grip rifles — originals were expertly shaped.

(ii) German Rifle Association insignia attached to the shell guard by means of two long pins — authentic badges were fixed in place by two short pins, or by a single rivet.

(iii) Lockets and chapes screwed into position — genuine mounts were stapled to the scabbard.

(iv) Chapes with ball tips — originals had flat terminals.

In the field of daggers, then, many anomalies exist and differentiating between original items and reproductions can be a perplexing business. Certain blades, eg those of the army and Reichsbahn, should have sharp ridges, while with others (SA, SS, NSKK etc) a sharp ridge is indicative of faking. Genuine Diplomatic Corps fittings were manufactured in silver plated brass, but Postschutz and Luftschutz daggers with components in silver plated brass are likely to be counterfeit. Red Cross hewer grips should be in plastic, not wood, whereas genuine forestry and hunting sidearms had grips in wood, not plastic. Original first pattern Luftwaffe daggers never had grip wire of a single twisted double strand, but Customs Service daggers always did. And so it goes on. Fortunately, however, there are other more general factors to be considered when examining pieces. These are outlined below.

ASSEMBLY

Original dagger assembly techniques differed from one pattern to another, but in all cases components fitted well together as quality control in German arms factories was meticulous, even during the last months of World War 2. Modern reproductions are no match for originals in this respect and so collectors must be wary of daggers with any misfitting parts. Blades should never be loose, like the one illustrated in **Plate 85**. Authentic pieces bearing large gaps between the pommel and the grip, or between the grip and the crossguard, would have been scrapped at once. Likewise, an SS grip with runes and eagle insignia lying in hollows far too large or too shallow to accommodate them (see **Plate 86**) would never have been passed by the SS/RZM inspectors. The collector's fundamental rule of thumb should be that if a dagger lacks refinement to such an extent that it would have shamed a Nazi uniform, then it is most probably a postwar copy.

Collectors should not be reluctant to strip pieces down prior to purchase, because internal examination plays a crucial part in fake detection. It is only by disassembly that the presence or otherwise of Diplomatic Corps and Government Administration numbers or of Eickhorn trademarks on the grips of TeNo hewers can be determined. Above all, inspection of the blade tang is most important since fake blades tend to be without the billet clamp seam, a ridge which ran along the sides of the vast majority of original tangs (see **Plate 87**). Genuine navy tangs were ground down to facilitate attachment of the crossguard retaining spring, however, so were minus the billet clamp seam. The same was true for Waterways Police daggers, German Rifle Association sidearms, and most swords, which required slightly curved tangs and so had their seams ground off during assembly.

MARKINGS

A wide variety of marks, both etched and stamped, featured on Third Reich daggers and many have been reproduced. The most common was the maker's mark, ie the manufacturer's trade emblem, which normally appeared on the upper reverse blade. There were over 100 different producers of edged weapons and certain businesses had more than one trademark, so the variation in logos which may be encountered by collectors is enormous. However, all genuine marks were well defined, unlike the typical fake representations which tend to be sketchy in appearance (see **Plate 88**). With the notable exception of the Karl Burgsmüller NPEA daggers, any daggers purporting to emanate from Berlin should be viewed with particular suspicion, since 'Berlin' frequently replaces 'Solingen' on reproduction trademarks as a convenient way of circumventing the copyright restrictions protecting their original counterparts.

The producers of NSDAP daggers came under the authority of the RZM and, after 1935, daggers manufactured on a large scale for general issue to members of the SA, SS, NSKK and Hitler Youth each bore the maker's RZM code number in lieu of his trademark. Special presentation daggers, however, or items which had to be purchased privately such as the SS 1936 chained dagger, were normally contracted out to a few prestigious makers and they continued to carry trademarks, or were completely unmarked. Wehrmacht and other non-political daggers were never RZM marked either, and any such piece sporting an RZM code number is likely to be a fake.

Centrally issued, as opposed to privately purchased, SA, SS and NSKK daggers were stamped on the reverse lower crossguard with a Gruppe mark which identified the territorial district responsible for issuing the dagger. While the presence of a Gruppe mark is no guarantee of authenticity, most fakes omit this feature (see **Plate 89**). Stamped or engraved serial numbers were also used for accountability purposes with

certain issue daggers, particularly those of the Luftwaffe, NPEA, Postschutz and TeNo. The serial number was most commonly found on the crossguard or the blade itself, with a matching number on the scabbard locket (see **Plate 90**). Again, these marks are normally absent from reproductions.

A very few army, navy and Luftwaffe daggers were stamped with the Waffenamt symbol, comprising a small eagle and swastika, the letters 'Wa A' and a serial number which showed that they had been inspected and had met with Wehrmacht quality control requirements (see **Plate 91**). This feature was extremely rare, however, as the majority of dress daggers were bought privately by Wehrmacht personnel and not issued by armed forces quartermasters.

ENGRAVING AND ETCHING

Fakers have for long 'enhanced' original Nazi daggers by the application of elaborate postwar designs and dedications, which may be either engraved or etched. Pieces so altered are then offered as unique 'honour daggers' or 'presentation blades', and can fetch two or three times the price sought for a basic, unembellished dagger. The major factor to consider when examining ornamentation like this is quality: most reproductions simply fail to come up to the standard of workmanship required during the Third Reich.

The original use of engraving tended to be confined to 'one-off' presentation pieces, although it was also favoured by many dagger owners who had their names or initials put on the crossguard reverse for identification purposes. Inscriptions such as these were executed by local jewellers. Any engraving, therefore, which is not professional in appearance, or which has not aged with the rest of the dagger, is likely to be a modern addition.

Etching, on the other hand, was a standard feature of many Nazi daggers and a wide range of genuine patterns and finishes was produced. Some etchings, for example, had light grey coloured backgrounds to their designs, while others had recesses which were almost black. The etched mottoes on

SA, SS, NSKK and NPEA daggers were, however, alike in that they were always sited much closer to the hilt than to the tip of the blade. Unfortunately, fakes of every type of etching exist. Points to be especially wary of are:

(i) Incomplete, deformed or uneven etching — all patterns should be crisp, symmetrical and flawless. Lettering with chunks missing, or with ragged outlines, would never have been allowed to leave any Nazi blade factory (see **Plate 92**).

(ii) Stippling, ie small raised 'dots', either on the etching itself or to the background area — genuine etching was always smooth.

(iii) Painted lettering — fake SA and RAD sidearms have been encountered with their etched mottoes painted brown as a means of camouflaging the stippling described above. Many bear the trademark 'Gebrüder Heller, Schmalkalden'. Paint was never applied to original blades.

As well as reproductions of authentic designs, various completely fanciful etchings have appeared on many pieces in recent years. These include a number of so-called

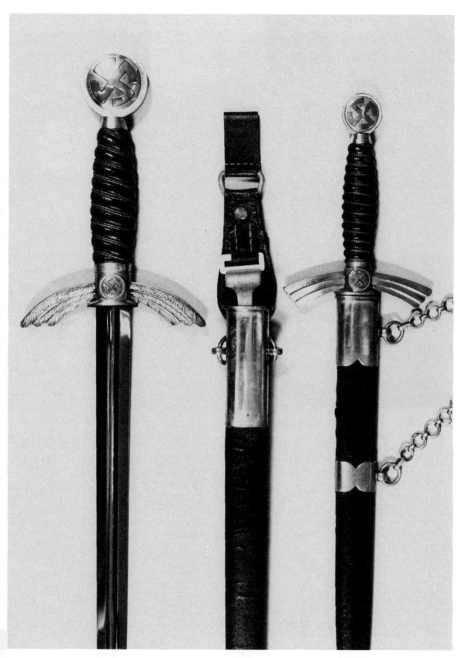

Plate 84 Luftwaffe Sword and 1935-Pattern Dagger: *both originals and both by 'SMF'. The Luftwaffe sword was by far the most expensive standard issue sword produced during the Third Reich (at RM 32, almost double the price of the army counterpart), and its high quality finish and leather fittings have precluded any attempts at faking.*

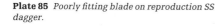

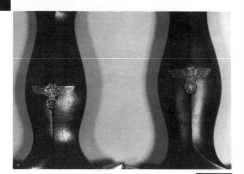

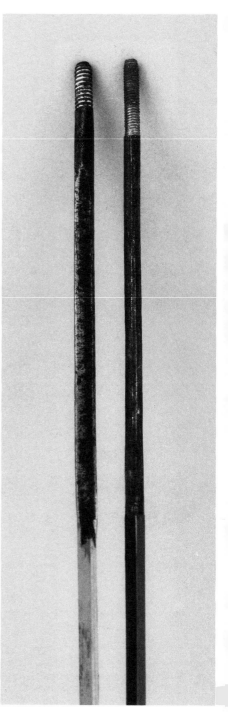

Plate 85 *Poorly fitting blade on reproduction SS dagger.*

Plate 86 SS Grip Eagles: *original (left) and fake (right). The original is die-struck German silver and neatly attached to the grip by means of two prongs. The copy is crudely cast, its wings are too square in shape, and it is glued into a hollow which has been cut too large and too high up the grip.*

Plate 87 Blade Tangs: *reproduction (left) and original (right). Note the billet clamp seam, evident on the original but not present on the fake.*

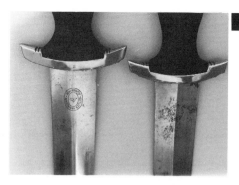

Plate 88 Etched Makers' Marks: *original (left) and fake (right). The original is crisply executed while the copy is less clear.*

Plate 89 *The original SS dagger (left) clearly has the Gruppe mark 'III' (Gruppe Spree) stamped into the reverse of the crossguard. The fake (right) is minus this feature.*

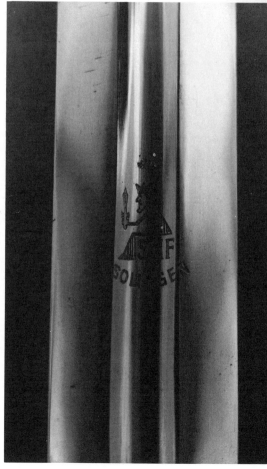

Plate 90 *Matching unit stamps on the blade and scabbard locket of an original Luftwaffe 1935-pattern dagger. Such marks are not usually present on reproductions.*

Plate 91 *The stamped Waffenamt symbol is just visible above the etched maker's mark 'SMF' on this Luftwaffe blade.*

'SS Presentation Bayonets' which are in reality standard army issue M84/98 service bayonets, or dress bayonets, with spurious etchings applied. The inscriptions are generally quite meaningless: 'SS Adolf Hitler', 'Reichsmarschall', 'Wallenstein', 'Siegfried' and 'SS Totenkopfwachsturmbann Sobibor' are examples. Covered with over-sized siegrunes and morale-boosting slogans, these bayonets are base in the extreme and are instantly recognisable by virtue of their inherent vulgarity.

'FANTASY' DAGGERS

The lowest of the low, so far as purists are concerned, are the so-called 'fantasy' daggers, which cannot be classed even as reproductions since they have no original counterparts. A few of these fantasies comprise various combinations of reworked dagger parts, both genuine and fake, Nazi and otherwise, and are in themselves visually attractive propositions. Others, such as the 'Reichskanzler Adolf Hitler' and 'Deutschland Erwacht' penknives, which were struck in the 1970s from previously unused dies produced in 1933 by the J. A. Henckels firm, have some historical basis. The majority, however, are made from scratch, the raw results of over-active post-1945 imaginations. The 'SS-Streifendienst Pantograph Knife', for instance, and the 'Belt Buckle Dagger', examples of which suddenly flooded the market in the 1970s, represent all that is bad in the fantasy. Crude in design, construction and quality, it is inconceivable that anything remotely like them would have seen the light of day in Hitler's Germany. In a similar vein, modern sheath-knives with cast copper eagles on the grip and etched swastikas on the blade, and old bayonets and fighting knives with new SS runes badges glued to the handle, have been sold side by side as 'rare prototypes' and 'important finds'. Crude fakes such as these should always be avoided unless the enthusiast wishes to utterly debase his collection.

92

Plate 92 SS Blade Etching: *original (above) and fake (below). The original etching is crisp and central to the blade. The fake is less deeply executed and off-centre, rising from left to right in the photograph.*

3 Headgear

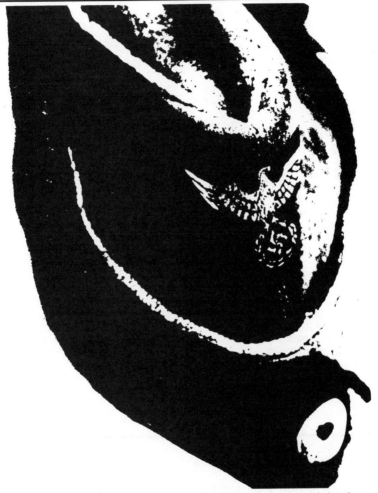

The faking of Third Reich headgear can be classified into three main groups, ie steel helmets, peaked caps and field caps. Methods used to detect reproductions vary accordingly.

Despite the fact that all Nazi steel helmets are in great demand, little or no attempt has been made at serious out-and-out reproduction of helmets. Costs would be prohibitive and, in any case, original examples are still readily available. The decals worn on helmets have, however, been widely copied and it is commonplace for genuine army helmets to be adorned with fake decals pertaining to other formations, particularly the SS. Such helmets are then sold at prices three or four times as high as they would have fetched originally.

Genuine Third Reich decals were each applied by hand to the helmet surface using Ducolux, Kopal or Damar lacquer, which was allowed to dry for a full hour before the paper backing was removed from the decal. After a further 24 hours had elapsed, the decal was coated with a protective layer of lacquer which rendered it very resilient to wear and impervious to the elements. Indeed, in 1943, when all decals were ordered to be removed from combat helmets for the duration of the war, many soldiers found that their decals were so adhesive that they could not be detached, even by the most persistent scraping. The only way to eradicate them was to repaint the helmet!

Fake decals are far inferior in quality to the real thing. They are normally applied in much the same way as model aircraft decals, ie by soaking in water and transferring directly on to the helmet. Many are inaccurate in size and specification, most lack detail, and all can be scratched off with the slightest pressure from a finger nail. Reproduction decals can also be detected as such by the simple fact that they tend to be unblemished while the helmet to which they are attached shows signs of natural ageing and wear, even if it has recently been resprayed. Some fakers have scored away sections of newly-applied decal in an attempt to make the item in question look much older than it really is, but no amount of artificial distressing can quite 'weather' a helmet decal to the same extent as the passage of time.

Plates 93 to **99** illustrate a selection of original and fake decals and should give the reader a good idea of what to look out for.

The modern West German Border Guard helmet is based on the Wehrmacht 1935 pattern but is easily identified by the fact that, unlike its Nazi counterpart, its liner is secured by means of a single bolt at the top of the helmet, rather than three split pins around the sides. Collectors should bear in mind, however, that original Third Reich civil helmets were far less standardised than those of the military and featured many variations in the shell, liner and even chinstrap arrangement (see **Plate 100**).

Finally, camouflage cloth helmet covers have been widely faked, especially those of the Waffen-SS. These copies occasionally make use of genuine war surplus material, but are consistently let down by their blackened brass retaining clips. Originals, such as that illustrated in **Plate 101,** had retaining clips in blackened steel, aluminium or zinc alloy.

PEAKED CAPS

The quality of original Nazi peaked caps varied greatly. Issue caps tended to be manufactured from a rather basic woollen material, but wearers of all ranks had the opportunity to purchase one or more of a gradation of finer caps which were produced by specialist tailors and hatters. The buyer could have his cap crown and body done in lightweight ribbed twill or moleskin, and his cap band in wool or velvet, depending upon how much he was prepared to spend. Interior fittings ranged from harsh hessian linings and pressed paper sweatbands to exquisite silk linings complemented by sweatbands in soft leather. Peaks were almost universally of vulcanised fibre, with a shiny black coating and a raised rim around the edge to give strength. A semi-

Plate 93 Model 1935 Steel Helmet: *original. This early double decal helmet was found in Norway in 1975 and was undoubtedly used in the Norwegian campaign of 1940. Its well-worn appearance is enhanced by the fact that the original owner painted the helmet white during his service in snow-covered terrain and thereafter applied a coat of matt grey paint when he returned to a more temperate area. Both layers of paint have been worn through time and partially removed to reveal the Wehrmacht eagle decal, shown, and the national shield decal on the right-hand side. No matter how the fakers try, they cannot duplicate this sort of weathering which is apparent on almost all original helmets.*

Plate 94 Luftwaffe Eagle Decal: *original. This illustrates the high quality of detail which was embodied in wartime decals, and shows how resilient they were to wear and tear. The helmet has been well used, but the decal remains almost intact.*

Plate 95 National Shield Decal: *original. In this case, the decal is bubbled due to the retaining lacquer not having been spread properly, or the decal not having been smoothed out sufficiently during application. Nevertheless, the flawed decal is still adhering to the helmet 50 years later — something modern fakes could never do.*

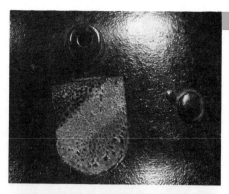

Plate 96 SS Decal: *original. The helmet has clearly seen some considerable front-line service, and the decal was sturdy enough to withstand it. Scores and marks on the paintwork of the helmet can be seen to continue into the battered decal. Each rune measures 6mm in width and 24mm in length, as opposed to the fake SS decal shown in* **Plate 98**.

Plate 97 Army Helmet Decals: *reproductions. All types of helmet decals have been faked, and those illustrated are typical. They are on a paper backing and are applied in much the same way as model aircraft decals, ie they are removed from the backing by soaking in water and are then transferred directly on to the helmet. The national shield decal at left is of the correct size (33mm × 40mm), but the Wehrmacht eagle decal is too large at 35mm × 43mm.*

97

96

98

99

Plate 98 SS Decal: *fake. This 1934-pattern helmet, used by the Police, Fire Brigade and other uniformed non-combatant organisations, has had a fake SS decal applied so that it can be sold as an 'SS Lightweight Parade Helmet', or an 'SS Barracks Fire Brigade Helmet'. The paintwork on the helmet has worn with age, whereas the decal is absolutely unblemished — an instant giveaway. Moreover, the decal is very fragile and can be scraped off with slight pressure from a finger nail. The decal is not even accurate in its proportions — the runes are 7mm in width by 23mm in length and fairly 'stubby' in appearance when compared to the original illustrated in* **Plate 96**.

Plate 99 Swastika Decal: *original (above, on helmet) and fake (below). Note that the fake swastika is too thin, off-centre and rectangular rather than square. The shield itself is far too large at 34mm × 45mm.*

Plate 100 Variant Chinstrap Buckle: *original. Fire Brigade helmets bearing chinstrap buckles such as this one are often discounted as fakes because the buckle is of the 'briefcase-type' and totally unlike anything encountered on Nazi armed forces helmets. However, the buckle illustrated is entirely original and was patented during the Third Reich (patent no KA-1794) for its 'quick-attachment, quick-release' capability, ideal for use by fire fighters.*

Plate 101 Waffen-SS Camouflage Helmet Cover: *original. The cover illustrated is an early one, produced before foliage loops were introduced in 1941. It is of the 'Plane Tree No 1' pattern and is waterproof and summer/winter reversible. The summer side with green, brown and pale purple hues is shown, the reverse being brown and orange in colour. Spring clips situated on each side and at the rear are of blackened steel with bare aluminium 'U'-shaped hooks and secure the cover to the helmet. The clips on this example are retained in place by small blackened steel rivets, in accordance with the original patent drawings of February 1937. These rivets were replaced by larger, more robust aluminium ones on later production helmet covers.*

101

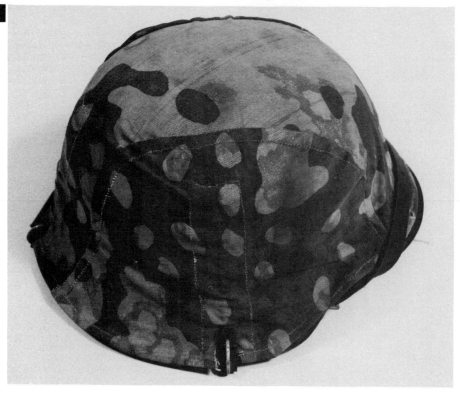

102

103

4

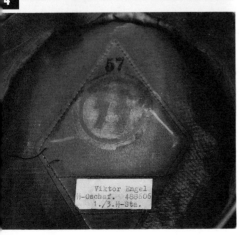

Plate 102 Peaked Caps: *reproduction Waffen-SS officer's cap (left) and original army officer's cap (right). The fake is a modern West German army peaked cap which has had its Federal insignia removed and replaced by good quality reproduction SS badges. Its overall appearance is very convincing indeed and it would be virtually undetectable as a fake without internal examination. Even the colours and piping are correct, although the cap band is in black wool rather than the black velvet which was characteristic of original SS officers' caps.*

Plate 103 Peaked Cap Sweat Shield: *fake. The sweat shield illustrated is stitched inside the reproduction Waffen-SS officer's cap shown in* **Plate 102***. The maker's trade mark and details are similar in style to those which may be found on original sweat shields, but the mass of code numbers and the soft, pliable plastic nature of the shield are typically West German. The numbers denote that this item was manufactured in 1973. '59' is the cap size.*

Plate 104 Peaked Cap Sweat Shield: *original. This sweat shield forms part of an Allgemeine-SS man's peaked cap. It is in a semi-brittle celluloid which is difficult to double back on itself and which is prone to splitting. Such stiff celluloid shields were common to all original Third Reich peaked caps, manufactured during a period when soft, pliable plastic of the type used to make the sweat shield illustrated in* **Plate 103** *had not been developed. Note also the SS proof mark in gold impressed into the crown beneath the shield, and the paper insert bearing the owner's name, rank, SS number and unit.*

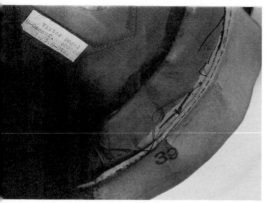

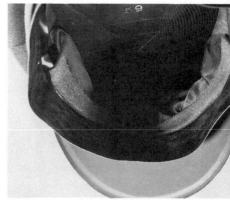

105

106

107

Plate 105 Peaked Cap Sweatband: *original. This upturned sweatband is of the wartime ersatz type in pressed paper. Note how the hessian lining is loosely hand-stitched into position behind the sweatband. Modern West German peaked cap linings are neatly machine stitched into place.*

Plate 106 Peaked Cap Interior: *reproduction. Another view of the fake Waffen-SS cap shown in* **Plate 102**. *Note in particular the giveaway plastic foam sponge padding. The sweatband is of polyurethane, vinyl-like in appearance, and the shiny nylon lining is neatly machine stitched behind a plastic beading strip around the sweatband. It is interesting to note that this piece has a label attached to the cap spring which reads, 'Hier ziehen! Lagerbügel herausnehmen!' ('Pull here to remove storage hoop'). Obviously, West German army officers still have a penchant for the 'crusher look'!*

Plate 107 Peaked Cap Interior: *original. The sweatband is of soft fine grain leather and the high quality silk lining is loosely hand-stitched behind it. Note that there is no foam padding or plastic beading in evidence.*

Plate 108 Chin Cords: *reproduction. The large, square knotted slider to the chin cord illustrated has as its base a flattened oval tube made from rigid white plastic, denoting it as being of modern manufacture. Wartime sliders had their base tubes in steel, tin, zinc or stiffened leather.*

108

brittle transparent celluloid sweat shield was stitched inside every cap crown, and it featured a slot into which the owner of the cap could place a tag bearing his name, for identification purposes. In addition, the shield normally carried the particulars of the hat size and/or the manufacturer.

Reproduction Third Reich peaked caps usually comprise modern West German military or Police caps, which have had all Federal insignia removed and replaced by genuine or fake Nazi badges. Externally, these fraudulently altered items are generally of very good quality and most convincing (see **Plate 102**), but internally they can be readily distinguished by their having one or more of the following characteristics:

(i)   Soft, pliable plastic sweat shields, like that illustrated in **Plate 103** — originals were in semi-brittle celluloid only, as in **Plate 104.**

(ii) Nylon linings neatly machine-stitched into place behind the sweatband — instead of the authentic silk, artificial silk or hessian-type linings which were loosely hand-stitched into position on originals (see **Plate 105**).

(iii) Polyurethane sweatbands with a vinyl-like appearance — genuine examples were in leather or pressed paper.

(iv) Plastic foam padding in the cap body (see **Plate 106**) — never a feature of originals (see **Plate 107**).

(v)   Chincords with plastic components, such as that illustrated in **Plate 108** — genuine components were in steel, zinc or stiffened leather.

(vi) Plastic chinstraps — these should be of leather or pressed paper.

(vii) Plastic peaks — originals were in vulcanised fibre or leather.

(viii) Modern synthetic thread — all original stitching should be in cotton.

(ix) The West German government approval mark 'DBGM' — the Nazi equivalent was 'DRGM'.

To complicate matters, however, numerous original peaked caps have been 'doctored' to pass as scarcer versions and these frauds, of course, display none of the aforesaid West German features. Methods used by the faker to convert an everyday item into a desirable rarity are often quite simple, normally involving a touch-up with a felt-tipped pen, and sometimes a change of insignia. Several army infantry officers' peaked caps, for example, have had their white piping coloured pink by means of a marker pen and have thereafter been sold as scarce 'panzer officers' caps'. When purchasing rare caps then, the collector should be on the lookout for marks made by previously attached insignia, and should closely examine the piping and other areas for signs of recolouring. Original piping will be coloured the same throughout its length and width. Any piping which shows a white backing, or has variations in colour that are not of the piping's base colour, should be viewed with alarm. Piping should also be cleaner under the sides of the cap than along the front or back. Protected by the overlapping body of the crown, such piping will not have been exposed to the sun or to the elements and will show a truer and darker colour. Piping that does not show these colour variations may be suspect.

FIELD CAPS

Original Nazi field caps, such as the one illustrated in **Plate 109,** were always produced to a high standard, irrespective of the type of cap or rank of the wearer. Many modern West German and foreign military and police field caps have been altered to pass as Third Reich examples, but these are generally inaccurate in style and are not too difficult to detect (see **Plate 110**). Collectors should be particularly wary of the following features:

(i)   Marks left by the removal of Federal or non-German insignia.

(ii) Nylon linings, plastic sweat shields, polyurethane sweatbands and spurious markings — original field caps had plain twill linings, without

Plate 109 Army Officer's 1938-Pattern Field Cap: original. The cap body is in fine moleskin material with aluminium piping around the crown and upper edge of the frontal scoop.

Plate 110 1943-Pattern Field Caps: reproduction (left) and original (right). The reproduction is in fact a modern West German Border Guard's cap with Federal insignia removed and fake Nazi eagle and national cockade, crudely embroidered on a dark green felt triangle, added. The cap is in a dark green ribbed twill material with false turn-ups and bottle-green piping around the crown. The two frontal buttons are dark grey alloy. The original cap is in soft field grey wool with serviceable turn-ups allowing the sides to be pulled down around the ears. There is no piping to the crown and the buttons are in field grey painted zinc. Insignia is BEVo woven and machine-stitched to the cap.

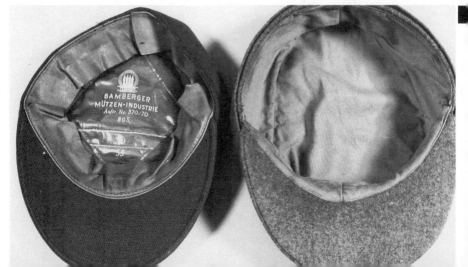

Plate 111 *Interiors of items shown in* **Plate 110.**
*The fake cap (left) has a nylon lining, grey
polyurethane sweatband with plastic beading
strip, and a sweat shield in soft, pliable plastic. As
well as the maker's details, the sweat shield bears
the code markings, 'Auftr. No. 370/70' ('Order No.
370 of 1970') and 'BGS' ('Bundesgrenzschutz' —
'Federal Border Guard'). The original (right) has a
rough twill lining, without sweat shield or
sweatband. This example is unmarked, although
many originals bore RB code numbers in black ink.*

Plate 112 *Panzer Field Caps: reproduction (left)
and original (right). The film prop fake purports to
be a 1940-pattern field cap for Waffen-SS tank
crews. It is, in reality, a 1960-period French
Foreign Legion forage cap in heavy black wool with
red piping, to which has been added SS eagle and
totenkopf insignia poorly embroidered in white
cotton on a back felt base. The original at right is a
scarce example of the 1940 airman's cap in black
ribbed twill, worn by members of the Luftwaffe
Panzer Division 'Hermann Göring'. The insignia
are finely machine-embroidered on black wool.*

Plate 113 *Interior of reproduction SS field cap
shown in* **Plate 112.** *The stamp of the French maker
is clearly visible.*

Plate 114 *Army Officer's Field Cap Interior:
original. This photograph shows the inside of the
front of the cap illustrated in* **Plate 109.** *A private
purchase piece, it has a fine quality silk lining and
a small, soft leather sweatband.*

sweat shields or sweatbands, except for a few officers' privately purchased types which had silk or artificial silk linings, brittle celluloid sweat shields and leather or pressed paper sweatbands (see **Plates 111 to 114**).

(iii) Synthetic thread — authentic stitching was in cotton.

(iv) 'DBGM' approval marks — instead of the proper 'DRGM' or 'RB' marks.

(v) Post-1945 date and issue stampings — incredibly, these are often left intact on 'doctored' West German caps!

As with peaked caps, many original but common field caps have been altered to look like rarer versions. Some army caps, for example, circulate with SS badges attached, and these are identifiable as such only by the newness of the stitching securing their replacement insignia. Others have been dyed black to pass as much-sought-after panzer caps, although their linings usually end up being dyed as well, which was not the case with originals. Even old items of civilian headgear, like that illustrated in **Plates 115** and **116,** have been 'Nazified' by the addition of appropriate insignia. The permutations are almost endless. In general terms, however, all component parts of any given piece of headgear should show equal signs of age and wear, and that applies as much to original wartime 'conversions' as it does to regulation items. If an unissued cap has spent the last 50 years in a box, all parts will be near mint; if an issued cap was worn for a prolonged period, all parts will be weathered. It follows that any old cap offered with new-looking badges, or vice versa, is almost certain to be a postwar 'mock-up'. Even if the component parts are authentic, the whole will always lack the desirability of a completely untouched wartime piece and would really best be avoided by the serious collector.

115

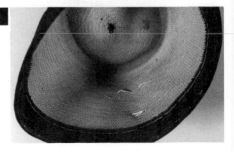

116

Plate 115 Waffen-SS Dress Fez: *fake. This item is very convincing, being an old and naturally aged civilian fez in heavy maroon wool with a black silk tassel. The badges are good quality reproductions.*

Plate 116 *Interior of item shown in* **Plate 115**. *The bare straw base exposes this fez as being of a basic civilian type. Original SS issues were lined with field grey twill and had leather or pressed paper sweatbands.*

4   Tunics

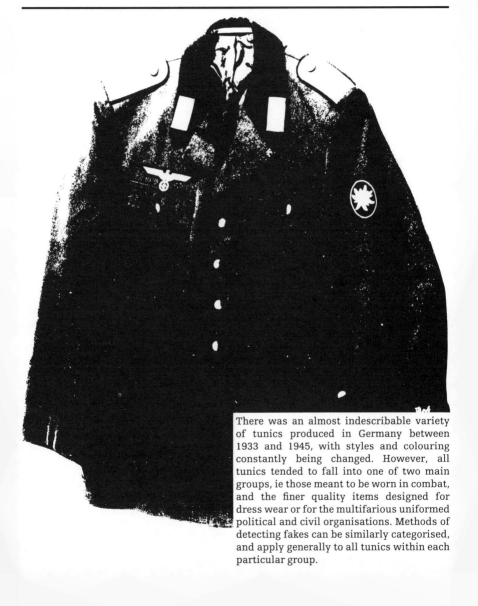

There was an almost indescribable variety of tunics produced in Germany between 1933 and 1945, with styles and colouring constantly being changed. However, all tunics tended to fall into one of two main groups, ie those meant to be worn in combat, and the finer quality items designed for dress wear or for the multifarious uniformed political and civil organisations. Methods of detecting fakes can be similarly categorised, and apply generally to all tunics within each particular group.

Reproductions of Third Reich combat tunics abound. Some were manufactured from scratch as film props, and these copies are not difficult to recognise since they were made to be viewed from a distance and only when being worn. They usually lack the more superficial characteristics such as linings, makers' marks, field dressing pockets, adjustable cuffs, belt hook eyelets and so on, which would not readily be missed 'on camera'. A few even have plastic buttons and bear crudely stencilled insignia. Their overall appearance is shoddy and would fool few collectors.

The majority of fake combat tunics, however, comprise modified West German military and police jackets, which closely parallel their predecessors in cut and are easily 'Nazified' by the addition of relevant insignia. Quality is generally very good, as the raw materials are professionally made tunics. Yet even these outwardly convincing counterfeits are readily identifiable if the collector keeps the following points in mind:

(i) All wartime field blouses, such as the one illustrated in **Plate 117**, were made from a coarse, heavy woollen/rayon cloth which has no modern West German equivalent. Federal issue jackets are manufactured from thinner lightweight ribbed synthetics, like polyester. **Plate 118** shows a typical West German conversion.

(ii) Original combat tunics were partially lined in rough cotton twill or artificial silk (see **Plate 119**), whereas post-1945 examples are fully lined in nylon (see **Plate 120**).

(iii) Nazi tunics featured holes at the waist to accommodate belt hooks. These are consistently absent from Federal jackets.

(iv) The 'closed collar', so typical of Third Reich field blouses, is no longer found on West German items which are all designed to be worn open at the neck.

(v) Authentic tunics usually had a distinctive 'zig-zag' pattern of under-collar stitching (see **Plate 121**), not encountered on modern jackets

because of changed manufacturing techniques (see **Plate 122**).

(vi) Most original combat tunics had their linings stamped with the maker's national factory code number, and size/date markings, in dark coloured ink. **Plate 123** illustrates a typical example. Some also bore unit issue details as shown in **Plate 124**. Fakes are invariably without these features.

(vii) The majority of genuine tunic buttons were in grey zinc alloy and were maker/date stamped. Only the last two numbers of the date were shown, eg '40' meant '1940', '41' meant '1941', and so on (see **Plate 125**). West Germany's accoutrement firms have continued this practice on their now standard issue silver plated brass buttons, so beware of postwar dates.

(viii) Look out for signs of Federal insignia having been removed to make way for Nazi badges.

(ix) Authentic stitching was in cotton, not synthetic thread.

In addition to copies of basic combat tunics, numerous fake camouflage items are in circulation. Waffen-SS smocks, in particular, have been widely reproduced, and since these often use material cut from original camouflage shelter quarters, the sole method of fake detection lies in the manner of their construction. The body of each original smock was produced from a single strip of material with a central hole to accommodate the head and neck, in poncho fashion. Consequently, the front and back comprised one continuous piece with no stitching from the neck across the shoulders to the top of each arm. Wartime smock sleeves were formed from two or three strips of material, made into 'tubes' and sewn together. Reproduction smocks are identifiable primarily by the fact that their bodies comprise two separate pieces of material, one front and one back, joined together by stitching across the shoulders. Moreover, their sleeves are generally made from a single strip of cloth rather than two or three 'tubes'.

Plate 117 Army Other Ranks' 1936-Pattern Field Tunic: original. Manufactured from a rough, hardy cloth mixture comprising 80% wool and 20% rayon, dyed field grey. This tunic, which bears the insignia of an artillery Kanonier, is a post-1940 example since the collar is also field grey rather than the earlier dark green. Note in particular the shape of the lapels, the belt hook holes and the lack of turnback cuffs. Each cuff is adjustable, with a 130mm split up the rear seam and a hidden button inside the wrist. External buttons are in bare grey zinc.

Plate 118 Army Other Ranks' 1936-Pattern Field Tunic: reproduction. This tunic is in fact a 1960s West German issue, 'Nazified' by the addition of relevant insignia, and is typical of its kind. It is manufactured from a lightweight ribbed synthetic polyester material in medium green, with a dark green woollen collar. The collar is not meant to be closed so a spurious set of chromium hooks have been added, one to the lower left lapel and one behind the upper right lapel, to facilitate this. There are no belt hook holes and the cuffs are of the turnback type, common to all West German tunics but reserved for officers during the Third Reich. Buttons are in silver plated brass. The collar patches and shoulder straps are Federal, and a fake eagle and swastika embroidered in white cotton on green felt has been stitched above the right breast pocket. The mountain troops' Edelweiss badge on the left arm is again of Federal design, as is the paratroop 'Fallschirm-Jäger Rgt.' cuff title. (The only Third Reich paratroop cuff titles read 'Fallschirm-Jäger Rgt. 1', 'Fallschirm-Jäger Rgt. 2' and 'Fallschirm-Division'.) The latter two insignia should be worn on the right sleeve, not the left, but in any case such a combination of badges is pure fantasy.

Plate 119 Field Tunic Interior: *original*. Note partial lining in rough cotton twill.

Plate 120 Field Tunic Interior: *reproduction. This illustrates the full lining in nylon common to West German tunics. Note that, as a combat tunic, it still retains a field dressing pocket, unlike the original dress item shown in* **Plate 130**.

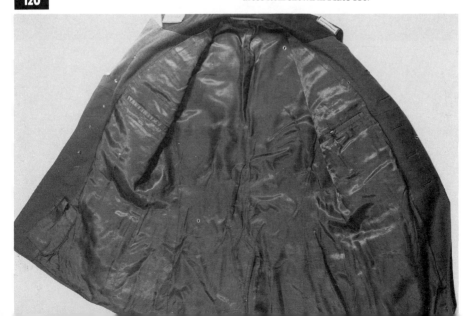

Plate 121 Tunic Collar: *original. The distinctive 'zig-zag' pattern of stitching invariably found on the underside of collars on original Third Reich tunics.*

Plate 122 Tunic Collar: *fake. The underside of a reproduction tunic collar reveals a complete lack of 'zig-zag' stitching.*

Plate 123 *RB code numbers stamped on an original field tunic lining.*

Plate 124 *Unit stores code numbers stamped on an original RAD tunic lining.*

Plate 125 Tunic Buttons: *original. Both are in grey zinc. The button on the left is from an NSDAP tunic and bears the maker's code number 'RZM M5/216' and logo 'OG'. That on the right is standard Wehrmacht issue, maker marked 'FLL'. Note in particular the date stamp '40', indicating manufacture in 1940.*

Plate 126 Waffen-SS 1944-Pattern Camouflage Field Tunic: *original. This item is in the so-called 'Pea' pattern camouflage design and is manufactured in printed lightweight herringbone denim, neither reversible nor water-repellent. The arm eagle is embroidered in light grey cotton on black wool.*

Plate 127 *Interior of item shown in* **Plate 126**. *Note lack of lining.*

Plate 128 Waffen-SS Italian Camouflage Field Tunic: *reproduction. After the Fascist collapse in 1943, Germany made a widespread use of discarded Italian camouflage material cut to German specification. The tunic illustrated is, however, of modern Italian army issue, characterised by its central and lower drawstrings and 'pop-stud' buttons. It has been enhanced by the addition of good quality fake insignia for an SS-Schütze of the 1st SS-Panzer Division, many of whose members wore Italian camouflage in Normandy in 1944.*

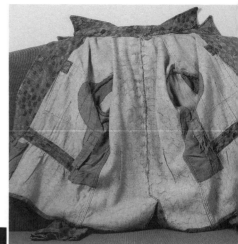

127

128

Waffen-SS camouflage tunics, such as the one illustrated in **Plates 126** and **127**, have not been seriously faked, but it is quite common for modern camouflage tunics to be adorned with reproduction SS badges and then be offered for sale as film props or even as 'variant' wartime pieces. They are, however, by their very nature, totally inaccurate in cut and materials and would not fool any but the most novice of collectors. **Plate 128** shows a typical example.

DRESS TUNICS

Reproductions of dress tunics, including those designed for daily wear by the various uniformed Nazi political and civil formations, once again generally take the form of altered West German items. At first sight these can be very convincing, particularly Luftwaffe types since the modern air force tunic is almost identical in cut to its wartime counterpart.

Moreover, the most glaring points of comparison which were used to recognise fakes in the field of combat tunics, ie the heavy coarse material and rough partial lining of originals as opposed to the fine material and full lining of West German conversions, are not so apparent in the realm of dress tunics where most original examples were also lightweight and fully lined. Even so, consideration of the following points should soon enable the reader to distinguish the spurious from the real thing:

(i)   Genuine dress tunics, such as that illustrated in **Plate 129**, were frequently tailor-made to individual order and were always of excellent quality. Federal issue jackets cannot match the originals in this respect.

(ii) Third Reich examples were manufactured in fine woollen-based cloth mixtures as opposed to polyester and other modern synthetics.

(iii) Originals were fully lined in real or artificial silk, or fine cotton twill, without any field dressing pockets (see **Plate 130**). West German tunics are fully lined in nylon, and frequently feature field dressing pockets since they were initially intended for general service wear.

(iv) The distinctive 'zig-zag' stitching pattern found under the collar of authentic tunics is not encountered on modern jackets.

(v)   Original dress tunics usually bore elaborate Third Reich tailors' labels, such as that illustrated in **Plate 131**, or, in the case of NSDAP items, RZM tags. Beware Federal government issue stampings or 'DBGM' markings in ink.

(vi) Watch out for signs of West German insignia having been removed, eg marks left by the cuff titles worn until recently on both sleeves of the modern Luftwaffe tunic.

(vii) All stitching should be in cotton, not synthetic thread.

Custom-made film prop copies of dress tunics, like those of combat tunics, are generally far less convincing than converted West German jackets and cannot stand up to even moderately close inspection. They were never intended to deceive, and few collectors would be taken in by them. **Plate 132** illustrates an original Allgemeine-SS service tunic and **Plate 133** shows a typical film prop version of the same item. Even from a distance, differences in cut, position of buttons, insignia and so on are self-evident.

Before concluding this section, three general points are worth mentioning. Firstly, all original uniform accessories were produced to the same high standard as the tunics which they complemented, and even neck ties were usually maker marked (see **Plate 134**). Any piece in synthetic materials or showing signs of shoddy workmanship is likely to be a reproduction. Secondly, large stocks of captured German tunics were purchased in 1945-46 by Allied film and theatrical companies and were subsequently marked 'Property of MGM', 'Ealing Studios', etc. Such markings, therefore, are not necessarily indicative of the film prop fake. Finally, collectors should be aware that

129

130

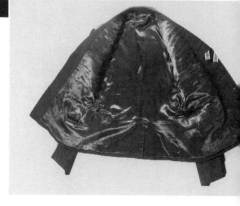

Plate 129 Luftwaffe Dress Tunic: *original. This
tunic was privately tailored in finely ribbed twill
for a Feldwebel of aircrew or paratroops. Quality is
superb.*

Plate 130 *Interior of tunic shown in* **Plate 129***.
Note full lining in silk, NOT nylon, and absence of
field dressing pocket as opposed to the faked
combat item shown in* **Plate 120***.*

Plate 131 Maker's Label: *original. This trade tag for the firm of 'K. Steffenauer, Aalborg', is one of a range of manufacturers' labels which may be encountered on original tailor-made dress tunics.*

Plate 132 SS 1932-Pattern Service Tunic: *original. Made of heavy black wool, this item bears the insignia of an SS-Mann serving with the 5th Company, 2nd Battalion, 4th SS-Foot Regiment (Hamburg-Altona). Note the 'slash' side pockets, two integral belt hooks, twill lining and RZM label. The armband is non-regulation, being of the standard NSDAP type rather than SS.* IWM MH16700

Plate 133 SS 1932-Pattern Service Tunic: *fake. This film prop is based on a modern British Police tunic, in fine serge with a nylon lining. The side pockets are of the 'patch' type and there are no belt hooks. A set of reproduction insignia for an SS-Mann in the Leibstandarte SS 'Adolf Hitler' has been added, but the shoulder straps are of the early field tunic variety rather than the single black and silver twisted cord type which was worn only on the right shoulder of the black tunic. Collar and collar patches are unpiped.*

dealers frequently 'upgrade' original tunics by attaching scarce insignia to them. A fairly common army infantry sergeant's field blouse, for instance, would be more saleable with a Demjansk Shield or a Tank Destruction Badge sewn into place. Where all such extra badges are genuine and compatible, there is little wrong with this procedure, provided the price asked for the final product does not exceed the total value of its individual components. However, many enthusiasts would consider that tunics so altered somehow lack the desirability of completely untouched wartime pieces.

Plate 134 *Linen RZM label sewn into the reverse of an original SA neck tie.*

134

5 Insignia

A vast array of insignia was created for wear by the military, paramilitary and civil organisations of the Third Reich. Badges can be classified into several types, and methods of fake detection vary from one type to another.

Metal badges were widely worn on all manner of Nazi headgear and tunics. The metal used in the production of such insignia varied considerably depending upon the date of manufacture, and included aluminium, brass, German silver, tombak, zinc and kriegsmetall. Early metal badges were plated, while later ones were merely dipped or hand painted in an appropriate colour. They could be crisply die-struck with a mirror-image appearance on the reverse, or finely cast with a smooth hollow back. Some had two or three round pins for attachment purposes, whereas others had flat prongs. Many bore makers' marks. All, however, had two things in common: a high quality finish and an inability to be bent without considerable pressure.

Reproduction metal badges have been on the market for many years and, fortunately, are for the most part easily spotted by virtue of their poor quality. The main give-away features are: construction from soft lead-based alloys which bend under the slightest pressure, or from brittle alloys which snap when pressurised; poor detailing, especially to eagles' eyes and wing feathers; unsubstantial prongs, needle pins or flat triangular tabs crudely soldered in place; deformed or ungeometric swastikas; unsightly markings caused by bad casting techniques; and spurious markings. The latest copies are die-struck in thin aluminium, and are fairly convincing, but still bend too easily.

Plates 135 to **141** illustrate a selection of original and reproduction metal insignia, for comparison purposes.

HAND-EMBROIDERED INSIGNIA

Hand-embroidered insignia were intended for officers and senior NCOs only, and were normally in a thick gilded or silvered 'bullion' or aluminium thread on a woollen base. The embroidery was done over cardboard templates, which could differ between manufacturing firms, resulting in many slight variations between badges of similar designs. Each completed piece had a heavy paper or soft linen cloth backing glued to its reverse to prevent the embroidery from fraying. Modern copies, many of which emanate from India and Pakistan, are characterised by their 'newness', lack of tarnishing or fraying, and their poor detailing with the usual uneven swastikas and so on. They are commonly on felt bases, and are either unbacked or backed with a thin grey synthetic paper fibre mixture or heavy black hessian totally unlike the paper or linen which featured on originals. **Plates 142** to **145** illustrate originals and copies. Beware items which smell of disinfectant. A dip in 'Dettol' is commonly used by fakers as a means of artificially ageing reproduction bullion badges.

MACHINE-EMBROIDERED INSIGNIA

Machine-embroidered insignia were made for wear by junior NCOs and other ranks. Manufactured on a large sewing machine-type device, using cotton thread on a woollen or woven base cloth, the final product had a raised effect. Colours could alter slightly from maker to maker, or from year to year, but all originals had heavy paper or soft linen backings to prevent fraying. Reproductions are usually crudely finished on felt, either unbacked or backed with a thin grey synthetic paper fibre mixture. The most recent copies are convincingly done on wool, but are again let down by their backings, in heavy black hessian. **Plates 146** to **149** show genuine and fake examples.

Plate 135 Army Peaked Cap Eagles: *original (above) and reproductions (centre and bottom). The original is cast in zinc with a white wash, dating it to 1942-45. Detail is well defined and it cannot be bent without considerable pressure. The copy at centre is die-stamped and of fairly good quality, with clear detailing, but is made from a very thin lead-based alloy which can be twisted out of shape by mere finger pressure. The fake at bottom is crudely cast in a brittle white metal alloy. Detail is indistinct and there are numerous pock marks over the surface of the badge.*

Plate 136 *Reverses of items shown in* **Plate 135**. *The original (top) has a smooth hollow reverse, typical of wartime castings, with two round pins soldered into circular recesses in the badge. The reverse of the copy at centre is also hollow, but with a mirror image of the obverse design and two flat prongs for attachment purposes. Many die-stamped originals also have this mirror image appearance, but are in far sturdier metals. The fake at bottom is solid with a flimsy needle pin assembly never used on genuine cap eagles.*

Plate 137 SS Cap Insignia: *all fakes. The eagle at top is a recent copy of the 1929-pattern NSDAP national emblem, die-struck in thin aluminium, easily bent, with black painted swastika. This form of eagle was seldom used after 1936, and the vast majority of originals were made of silver plated brass or tombak. A small number were struck in aluminium, but of a better quality which would not readily bend. The central eagle is a 1950s die-stamped tombak reproduction of the SS 1936-pattern national emblem. In this case, the eagle's head is deformed and the swastika is off-centre. The lower eagle is of the same pattern, but of 1970s manufacture and truer in form to the original. Once more, it is let down by the fact that is has been struck from a lead-based alloy which can easily be bent. The SS totenkopf at left is again in lead alloy, while that at right is the latest type of fake in aluminium. Both can readily be twisted out of shape. Original SS death's heads of this pre-1934 type were almost exclusively in silver plated brass or tombak.*

135

136

137

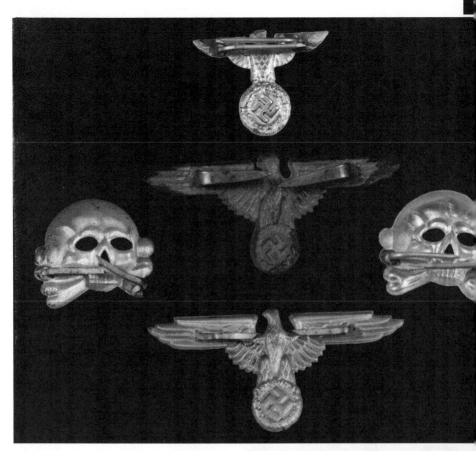

Plate 138 *Reverses of items shown in* **Plate 137**. *Note the wide triangular prongs on the eagle at centre, totally unlike anything which may be encountered on originals. The aluminium reproductions of the 1929-pattern eagle (top) and early totenkopf (right) are both unmarked with round pins while the lead-based fake totenkopf (left) and 1936-pattern eagle (below) have flat prongs on the reverse. The latter two badges are marked 'RZM 3/8' and 'RZM 40', respectively. Neither of these codes is in a form known to have been used during the Third Reich.*

Plate 139 SS 1934-Pattern Totenkopf: *original. This is a 1934-35 example in silver plated die-struck tombak, with exquisite high relief detailing. The hollow reverse has two flat prongs for affixing to the peaked cap and is stamped 'RZM M1/52', the code for Deschler & Sohn, München. From 1936, this pattern of skull was struck in aluminium then zinc alloy, and the RZM code numbers were replaced by SS/RZM contract numbers.*

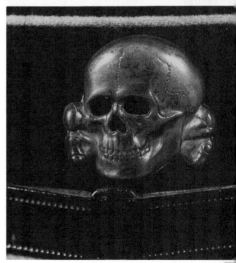

140

141

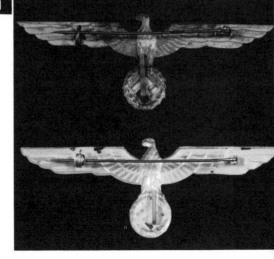

Plate 140 Army Summer Tunic Breast Eagle: *original (above) and reproduction (below). The original is die-struck tombak with a silver plating. The fake, in die-struck aluminium, is very convincing indeed and, apart from slight blurring of detail in places, its obverse cannot really be faulted. There is no doubt that it has been made to deceive and it would certainly fool many collectors.*

Plate 141 *Reverse of items shown in* **Plate 140**. *Note that the original (above) has a standard clip holding the needle pin in place, while the fake (below) has the pin secured by a modern brooch-type clip with integral safety catch.*

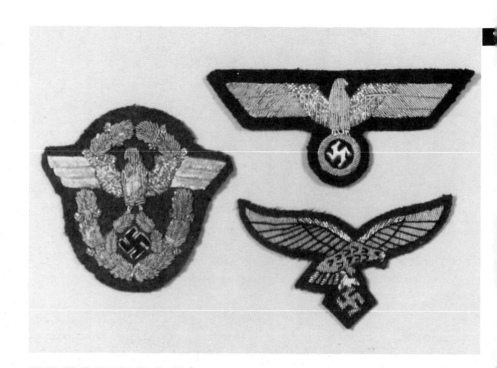

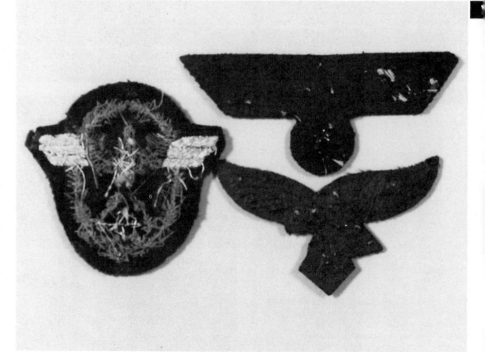

Plate 142 Bullion Insignia: *original Police officer's arm eagle (left) and fake army (top right) and Luftwaffe (bottom right) officers' breast eagles. The original at left is hand-embroidered in silver and aluminium bullion thread on a Police green woollen base. Workmanship is first rate and the black cotton swastika is symmetrical. The fakes are hand-embroidered on felt. Detail is distinctly lacking on the army eagle and has been crudely picked out in black thread on the Luftwaffe copy. Both reproductions have poorly formed swastikas.*

Plate 143 *Reverses of items shown in* **Plate 142**. *The original (left) has long since lost its paper backing but still remains intact. The fakes, on the other hand, need their paper backings to prevent their fragile felt bases from falling apart.*

Plate 144 WA Arm Badge: *original. This unusual item was worn on the left arm of the tunic by members of the WA ('Weer Afdeelingen' — 'Assault Detachment'), the Dutch Nazi Party's equivalent of the German SA. It was also worn by Dutch volunteers in the NSKK. It is hand-embroidered in gold bullion thread on a red and black woollen background. The central design is a 'wolfsangel' or 'wolf hook', used in various forms by the Nazis on all manner of insignia. Originally a mystical dark age Germanic talisman for warding off werewolves, the Wolfsangel was adopted as an emblem by 15th Century peasants in their revolt against the mercenaries of the German princes, and was thereafter regarded as being symbolic of liberty and independence.*

Plate 145 *Reverse of item shown in* **Plate 144**. *Note heavy paper backing and Dutch maker's stamp '161'.*

Plate 146 Luftwaffe Other Ranks' Breast Eagle:
*original (above) and fake (below). Both are
machine-embroidered in light grey cotton on a
blue-grey woollen base. The original has been cut
from a tunic, hence the narrow border. The
reproduction in this case is of excellent quality.
However, its swastika is too thin, the eagle's right
wing slopes generally downward rather than
upward, and the eye is picked out by a dot of black*
*thread. A whole series of these fake Luftwaffe
eagles has been produced, on blue-grey, tan, black,
white and green bases, and all bear the same three
flaws.*

Plate 147 *Reverse of items shown in* **Plate 146**.
*The original (above) has a soft linen backing to the
wool base while the fake (below) has a black
hessian backing.*

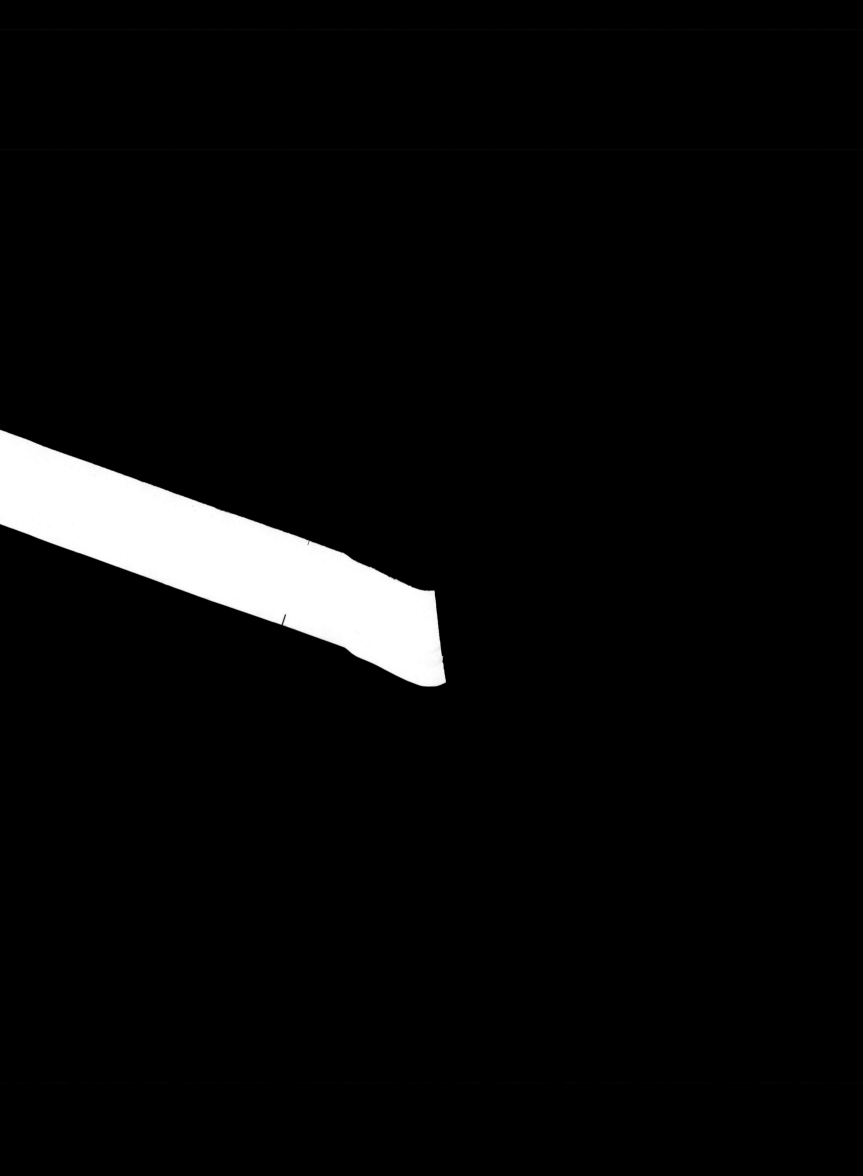

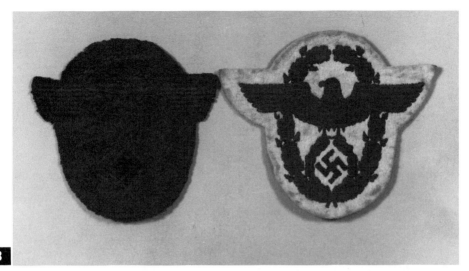

Plate 148 Police Other Ranks' Arm Eagle: *original (left) and reproduction (right). The original is machine-embroidered in bright green cotton on a medium green woollen base with black swastika, the colours of the Schutzpolizei, or Town Police. The fake is embroidered in red cotton on a white felt base, as worn on the Municipal Traffic Police white tunic. Note the distinctive form of the reproduction badge, in particular the pronounced oval shape of the oakleaf wreath, the acorns in silhouette, and the rounded head and short body of the eagle. A whole range of these fake Police eagles has been produced in the various departmental* colours and all feature the same characteristics. The design has also been used in a series of fake Police pennants, one of which is illustrated in **Plate 193**.

Plate 149 *Reverse of items shown in* **Plate 148**. *The paper backing has become detached from the original (left), but its heavy woollen base remains intact. The reproduction (right) is backed with a grey synthetic paper fibre mixture, glued into place to prevent the felt base from being teased apart during handling.*

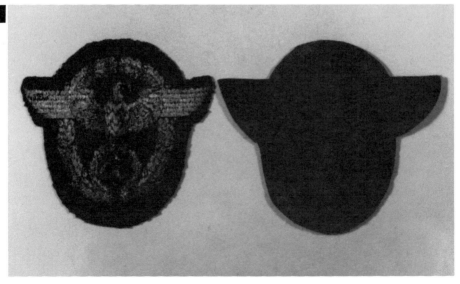

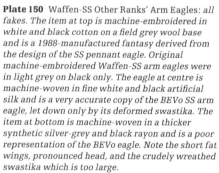

Plate 150 Waffen-SS Other Ranks' Arm Eagles: *all fakes. The item at top is machine-embroidered in white and black cotton on a field grey wool base and is a 1988-manufactured fantasy derived from the design of the SS pennant eagle. Original machine-embroidered Waffen-SS arm eagles were in light grey on black only. The eagle at centre is machine-woven in fine white and black artificial silk and is a very accurate copy of the BEVo SS arm eagle, let down only by its deformed swastika. The item at bottom is machine-woven in a thicker synthetic silver-grey and black rayon and is a poor representation of the BEVo eagle. Note the short fat wings, pronounced head, and the crudely wreathed swastika which is too large.*

Plate 151 *Reverse of items shown in **Plate 150**. The embroidered eagle at top is backed with a black hessian material. The item at centre, so convincing from the front, has on its reverse a rectangular 'block' weave pattern of a type never encountered on originals. The lower badge, on the other hand, while inaccurate in its design, has the correct weave pattern on the reverse.*

Plate 152 BEVo-Woven Army Breast Eagle: *original (above) and reproduction (below). The original is woven in dull mouse-grey on green artificial silk while the fake is in a shiny light grey on green synthetic material. The wreathed swastika is too large on the reproduction and the fake eagle's left wing is only 34mm in length as opposed to its right wing which measures 38mm.*

106

Plate 153 *Reverse of items shown in* **Plate 152**. *On the original (above) the eagle appears as a solid mass of silken threads whereas on the fake (below) a mirror image of the obverse design is clearly discernable.*

Plate 154 SS BEVo-Woven Cap Insignia: *both fakes. The upper badge is woven in a thick white synthetic thread on a black artificial silk base and is of the 1943 'economy' style with eagle and totenkopf featuring together on a triangular patch. The original form of this badge was not issued in great numbers, unlike the army equivalent, and is seldom seen in wartime photographs. Nevertheless, it has been extensively faked and many spurious variants, both woven and embroidered, are in circulation. Note the single row of teeth to the skull, characteristic of this reproduction. The lower totenkopf insignia is of superb quality and almost indistinguishable from the real thing. Woven in very fine artificial silk, the only giveaway is the pale yellow colour of the thread forming the skull, which should be in off-white or silver-grey. This item was cut from a roll containing hundreds of these near-perfect copies, so SS 'buffs' beware!*

Plate 155 *Reverse of items shown in* **Plate 154**.

Plate 156 SS BEVo-Woven Cap Insignia: *original.*
*The eagle is woven in off-white silk on black and is
far superior in quality and detailing to the fake
illustrated at the top of* **Plate 154**. *The totenkopf is
in off-white cotton on black artificial silk, but is
otherwise almost identical in form to the excellent
copy shown at the bottom of* **Plate 154**.

Plate 157 Police Sports Kit Insignia: *original.*
*BEVo-woven in green and black artificial silk on
white, and worn on the athletics vest or tracksuit.
A smaller, more oval version was produced for the
sports shorts.*

Plate 158 *Reverse of item shown in* **Plate 157**.

Plate 159 Waffen-SS Collar Patches: *original pair
(top) and two fake pairs (centre and bottom). The
originals bear the two rank bars of an
SS-Rottenführer but are of officer-quality
manufacture being hand-embroidered in fine
aluminium bullion thread on a soft, flexible velvet
base. It was not uncommon for junior NCOs to
wear officer-type badges, which they could
purchase at their own expense. The fake pair at
centre also depicts the rank of SS-Rottenführer,
but there all similarity to the original ends. The
runes are hand-embroidered in a bright, thick
silver bullion which is prone to tarnishing, are
mis-shaped with ragged edges and lie at the wrong
angle, while the rank bars are in a spurious twisted
silver bullion wire. The base is a heavy black
woollen material reinforced with cardboard so that
it does not bend easily. The pair of reproduction
collar patches at bottom, for the rank of
SS-Schütze, are excellent copies in the correct
black woollen cloth which was issued to other
ranks. The runes are machine-embroidered in light
grey cotton, as were originals of this type, but they
are too large, extending almost to the top and
bottom edges of the patch.*

Plate 160 *Reverses of items shown in* **Plate 159**.
*The originals (top) have the patch edges wrapped
around a fine canvas core, while the fakes at centre
are stiffly reinforced with cardboard. The
reproductions below have glossy white paper
centres over which the borders of each patch are
folded.*

MACHINE-WOVEN INSIGNIA

Flat machine-woven badges were worn extensively by all ranks. Very fine matt cotton and artificial silk threads were used for both the bases and the designs themselves, with thin aluminium wire for officer-quality insignia. The principal manufacturer of woven badges was the Wuppertal-Barmen firm of Bandfabrik Ewald Vorsteher, whose acronym 'BEVo' has come to be used generally when referring to all Nazi machine-woven insignia. Reproductions are of disturbingly good quality and, since originals did not have separate paper or linen backings, their reverses are in many cases indistinguishable from those of the real thing. The majority of known fakes, however, feature a rather thick shiny synthetic weave, disjointed swastikas, ill-defined eagles' beaks and minor errors in colouring, proportions and other design details (see **Plates 150** to **158**). In general terms, if a piece looks as if it could have been made yesterday, then it probably was!

SILK-SCREEN PRINTED INSIGNIA

From 1943, printing was used in the manufacture of national arm shields for wear by the Wehrmacht's foreign volunteers and Russian labourers working in Germany. Silk-screen operators ultimately produced vast quantities of these cheap badges on all sorts of backings and even army breast eagles and Waffen-SS sleeve eagles were being printed by the end of the war. There is no great demand for printed insignia and, apart from large numbers of rather dubious runic triangles as worn by foreign volunteers serving as SS-Helpers, the author is not aware of the existence of any fakes.

COLLAR PATCHES

Nazi collar patches varied in their quality and manufacture depending upon the rank of the wearer. Officers' patches were generally hand-embroidered in aluminium or gold bullion thread on a woollen or velvet base, while NCOs and other ranks wore patches machine-embroidered in cotton thread on a woollen base, or BEVo machine-woven in very fine matt cotton and/or artificial silk thread, either stitched to a woollen base or sewn directly on to the collar. Rank was commonly indicated by sturdy metal emblems mounted on to the standard woollen, velvet or artificial silk patches.

Reproduction collar patches usually have felt bases. The modern bullion thread which features on officer types is generally bright silver rather than dull aluminium, too new-looking and misshapen. Fake machine-embroidery tends to be excessively thin and sketchy in appearance, while bogus synthetic BEVo thread is too shiny and bulky in texture. Postwar copies of rank pips and of the various other metal emblems are invariably cast in soft, lead-based or brittle, glittery alloys. Waffen-SS collar patches are by far the most commonly reproduced type. **Plates 159** and **160** compare and contrast original and fake examples.

SHOULDER STRAPS

Third Reich shoulder straps came in detachable or sew-in varieties. Each officer-grade strap usually had an appropriately coloured woollen or velvet underlay over a cardboard base, with doubled or twisted aluminium top braid and plated alloy rank pips. The enlisted man's strap took the form of a cardboard base, which some makers chose to omit, covered with woollen cloth and an edging of woollen or silk waffen-farbe. Fake detection is fairly straightforward in this area, for reproductions are again characterised by their extensive use of felt instead of the proper materials (see **Plates 161** to **164**).

RANK CHEVRONS

All manner of rank and service chevrons have been copied, once more employing felt to imitate the appearance of the hardier wool or woven badge-cloth bases which featured on originals (see **Plate 165**).

UNIT CUFF TITLES

Unit cuff titles of every sort have been copied. However, it must be remembered that even the most widely distributed of originals, the 'Afrikakorps' title (see **Plates 166** and **167**), was superbly made and fakes are usually no match for the real thing in this respect. Again, beware of those constructed from felt.

The reproduction of both embroidered and woven SS cuff titles has been particularly prolific and lucrative and here quality is usually fairly good. Each machine-embroidered original comprised a 30mm-wide fine rayon strip, 500mm in length, with light grey cotton embroidery and borders of 14 aluminium threads (seven top and seven bottom). Very convincing fakes circulate in thicker rayon with borders of only 12 aluminium threads (six top and six bottom). Genuine BEVo-woven titles were in smooth artificial silk with an alternate black-and-white diced pattern along the reverse and loose vertical threads at the back of the wording. Copies of these have been produced in a rough cotton cloth with a tight weave behind the lettering. Many postwar fantasy pieces also exist, embroidered on black ribbon which was never used for this purpose during the Third Reich. **Plates 168** to **170** illustrate a selection of original and fake SS cuff titles.

ENAMELLED MEMBERSHIP BADGES

Every Nazi organisation had its own enamelled membership badge, the most common, of course, being that of the NSDAP itself. Such badges were almost exclusively die-struck from heavy tombak, with high quality enamel inlay on the obverse and silver or gold plating to the reverse and highlights. Examples dating from 1944-45 were in painted zinc.

All types of fake membership badge have

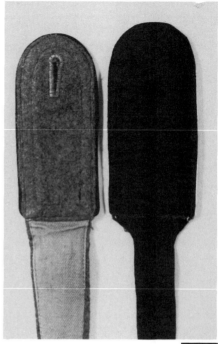

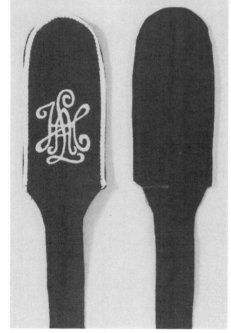

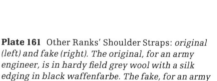

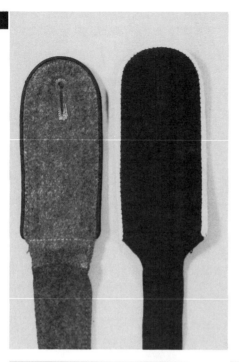

Plate 161 Other Ranks' Shoulder Straps: *original (left) and fake (right). The original, for an army engineer, is in hardy field grey wool with a silk edging in black waffenfarbe. The fake, for an army infantryman, is in bottle-green felt with white felt edging which can be easily pulled apart.*

Plate 162 *Reverse of items shown in* **Plate 161***. Note that the original strap (left) has a canvas backing to strengthen the tongue, while the fake (right) is all in felt.*

Plate 163 LAH Other Ranks' Shoulder Straps: *fake. These straps are once again made entirely from felt with the first pattern monogram of the Leibstandarte SS 'Adolf Hitler' machine-embroidered in white cotton on the upper side (left). The reverse (right) is plain. Similar monogrammed fakes have been produced for most elite units, including 'Feldherrnhalle', 'Grossdeutschland' and 'Führer-Grenadier-Bataillon'.*

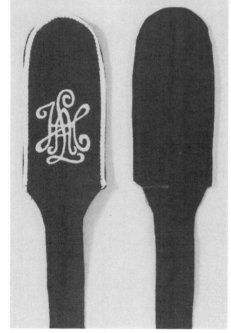

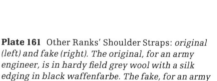

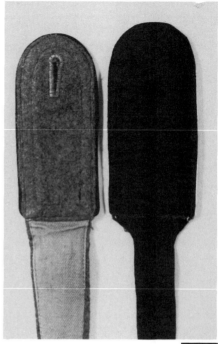

Plate 164 LAH Other Ranks' Shoulder Strap Tab: *original. This item features the second pattern LAH monogram, machine-embroidered in heavy grey cotton on a sturdy black woollen base.*

Plate 165 Rank Chevrons: *original (left) and reproduction (right). The original has a woollen base backed with linen, while the fake is on unbacked felt.*

Plate 166 'Afrikakorps' Cuff Title: *original. Note finely detailed machine-woven lettering.*

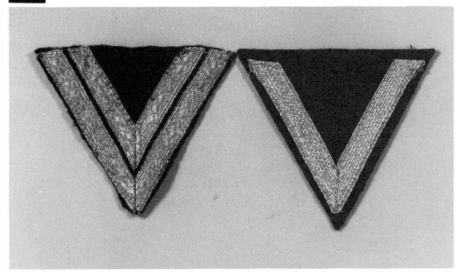

Plate 167 *Reverse of item shown in* **Plate 166**. *Note loose vertical threads behind the wording.*

Plate 168 SS Cuff Titles: all original. 'Reinhard Heydrich' and 'Westland' are of the machine-embroidered type and each has correct borders of 14 aluminium threads (seven top and seven bottom). 'Götz von Berlichingen' and 'Frundsberg' are BEVo machine-woven while 'SS-Polizei-Division' is an unofficial, hand-embroidered variant.   IWM MH7371

Plate 169 SS Cuff Titles: all fakes. 'Das Reich' is machine-embroidered in grey thread on black rayon in the correct manner, but has only six aluminium threads to each border, instead of

seven. In addition, the rayon is too heavy. 'Adolf Hitler' is expertly BEVo machine-woven in Sütterlin script, but on a rough cloth rather than the original artificial silk. Moreover, the 'up-stroke' is missing from the 'o' of 'Adolf'. 'Leibstandarte' is a complete fantasy piece machine-embroidered in silver bullion on black ribbon. Each border consists of nine aluminium threads. 'Britisches Freikorps' is another postwar fantasy, machine-embroidered in grey cotton on black ribbon with five tinsel-like threads to each border. It is 36mm in width rather than the correct 30mm. From a hazy wartime photograph, it is evident that cuff titles were produced for the few British volunteers in the Waffen-SS but that these pieces had the legend 'British Free Corps', ie in English, in a Gothic or copperplate script. The use of non-German languages on SS cuff titles was not unknown, one example being the titles produced for Dutch volunteers, some of which used the German word 'Niederlande' and others the Dutch form 'Nederland'.

Plate 170 *Reverse of items shown in* **Plate 169**. *The form of machine-embroidery apparent on 'Das Reich' is very close to the original but has rather too many loose threads extending horizontally between the letters. 'Adolf Hitler' has the correct alternate black-and-white diced pattern along the reverse, but with a tight weave at the back of the lettering whereas original BEVo titles had loose vertical silken threads there. 'Leibstandarte' has a strange backing of white cotton wool and 'Britisches Freikorps' has traces of dark grey cotton wool adhering to the reverse.*

⚡⚡Polizei-Division

Reinhard Heydrich

Westland

Götz von Berlichingen

Frundsberg

Das Reich

Adolf Hitler

Leibstandarte

Britisches Freikorps

115

Plate 171 NSDAP Membership Badges: *three originals (above) and one fake (below). The original at upper left is die-struck from tombak with high quality enamel inlay and silver plating, while that at upper centre, dating from 1944-45, is in painted zinc. The smaller variant original at upper right is also in finely enamelled tombak, but without the inscription around the border. The fake (below) is in die-struck aluminium and of very good quality. Note, however, that the swastika is too thin and the bare white lettering very pronounced. Of particular interest is the distinct space between the hyphenated 'L' and 'S' at the top left of the badge. Most reproductions seem to include this feature, while on originals the 'L' and 'S' tended to be placed much closer together.*

Plate 172 *Reverse of items shown in **Plate 171**. The original at top left is marked 'RZM M1/13' (L. Christian Lauer, Nürnberg) and that at top centre 'RZM M1/17' (F. W. Assmann & Söhne, Lüdenscheid). The variant at top right is unmarked and so it can be dated to pre-1935. It was probably made during the so-called 'verbotzeit' between 1923 and 1925 when the NSDAP and its uniforms and regulation badges were forbidden. The fake (below) is marked 'RZM M1/129', which was the code used during the Third Reich for the firm of Seiler & Co, Geldern. However, the RZM symbol is of the spurious type shown at (b) on **Fig 4**. The pin assembly is in soft aluminium, but very well formed.*

173

174

175

Plate 173 Danish Nazi Party Badge: *original. This stick-pin item struck in enamelled tombak and featuring a white swastika on a red background is strange in its design, but nonetheless original. It was worn on the left lapel by members of the DNSAP or 'Danmarks National-Socialistiske Arbejder Parti', the Danish equivalent of the NSDAP. It is a good example of an unorthodox piece of the sort which, without proper research, could well be dismissed out of hand as a postwar fantasy.*

Plate 174 SS Sponsoring Members' Badges: *original (above) and fake (below). The original is struck in silver plated and black enamelled tombak and is of the pattern worn by each of the 4,000 Belgian 'Beschermende Leden' who made regular financial contributions to the Germanic-SS in Flanders. Sponsoring Members, or 'Fördernde Mitglieder' were heavily relied upon by the SS to bolster funds during its infancy and the fake badge (below) is a good copy of the FM Decoration awarded to pre-1933 sponsors. Struck in black enamelled aluminium, it takes the form of the basic FM insignia with the addition of oakleaves and the inscription 'Dank der SS für Treue — Hilfe i.d. Kampfzeit' ('With thanks from the SS for loyal help in their time of struggle'). Originals of this award were produced in tombak.*

Plate 175 *Reverse of items shown in* **Plate 174**. *The original (above) is unmarked. The fake (below) bears the code number 'RZM M1/133', which was never used during the Third Reich. Moreover, the RZM symbol is of the reproduction type shown at (b) on* **Fig 4**. *The badge is also stamped with the serial number '3049', in an effort to make it appear as authentic as possible.*

117

been produced in lightweight aluminium. Quality is usually fairly good, although details are sometimes lacking and the enamel is often low-grade, bubbled, and easily chipped. Moreover, the markings on these badges are invariably inaccurate in form. **Plates 171** to **175** compare typical original and reproduction enamelled badges, while **Fig 4** shows what to look out for as regards markings.

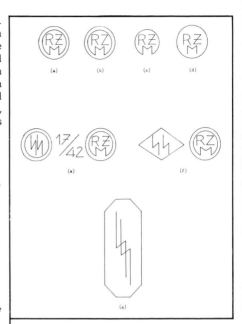

Fig 4 Original and Fake RZM and SS Proofmarks.

(a) *Original standard RZM proofmark with double circle, which appeared on all RZM-approved items, preceding the maker's code number. This style of mark has also been faked, particularly on daggers and paper labels.*

(b) *Fake version of (a), often encountered on reproduction badges such as those shown in* **Plates 172** *and* **175**. *Note that the 'Z' is minus its central stroke.*

(c) *RZM proofmark as at (a), but minus the outer circle. Genuine RZM marks on leather goods sometimes had to be of this type because of the difficulty of impressing a close double circle into heavy leather. However, this form of proofmark never appeared on original metal items or paper tags.*

(d) *Fake version of the RZM mark, without the inner circle.*

(e) *Original 'SS/RZM' proofmarks of the style used on SS items from 1936, when the SS began to contract out directly to RZM-approved firms without going through the RZM itself. The runes in double circle signifies SS approval of the manufacturer while the RZM proofmark indicates RZM approval. The number is that of the contract placed by the SS, and is used in lieu of the normal RZM contract number format. Once again, single circles frequently featured on leather goods because of stamping problems.*

(f) *Fake version of (e). The SS proofmark is in a diamond form, which was never the case with originals, and the 'Z' on the RZM proofmark is minus its central stroke. There is no contract number at all. This spurious type of marking features on the fakes shown in* **Plate 178**.

(g) *SS trademark used on original items such as dagger chains and sword mounts which were produced in SS-controlled factories rather than being contracted out to private commercial companies. This trademark was the idea of SS-Oberführer Professor Karl Diebitsch, who was responsible for the design of SS uniforms and insignia as well as being artistic director of the SS porcelain works at Allach. It is often confused with the SS proofmark shown at (e).*

6 Miscellaneous Regalia

Everything connected with the Nazi regime is collectable and so it has been profitable for fakers to reproduce sundry Third Reich regalia of all types on a grand scale. This section is devoted to such pieces.

Original Third Reich belt buckles can be categorised chronologically into four main types, ie those made of brass, steel, aluminium and kriegsmetall, and each type has its own peculiar reverse characteristics as shown in **Plate 176**. The earliest NSDAP buckles were made of brass, with plain buckle blanks to which were soldered thinly die-struck face plates bearing appropriate insignia. The reverse of the brass buckle was characterised by a semi-circular 'depressed slot' catch and signs of the soldering which secured the face plate to the blank. The 'post and prongs' arrangement used to attach buckle to belt took the form of a single piece of 'U'-shaped metal brazed to a tube, through which a retaining bar passed. These early buckles usually lacked makers' marks. Steel buckles, most of which were also unmarked, were much cheaper to produce than their brass counterparts and were generally die-struck in one piece to incorporate organisational insignia, with the reverse featuring a 'mirror' image of the obverse design. The 'depressed slot' catch was replaced by a 'C'-shaped bar brazed into position and the 'post and prongs' fitting had the 'U'-shaped piece of metal pushed through a sheet of tin which was then wrapped around the retaining bar to give a more stable arrangement than before. The majority of aluminium buckles were stamped or cast in a single piece, although a few cheaper Wehrmacht versions comprised plain buckle blanks with thin face plates attached by four edge tabs. The reverse of the standard aluminium buckle bore a novel form of catch, being a high-relief bulge or protuberance in the metal with a slot drilled through it. Most cast aluminium buckles also featured makers' details as integral parts of their reverse designs. The final manufacturing technique to appear before the end of the war was injection moulding using the ubiquitous zinc-based kriegsmetall. The reverse of the zinc buckle was typically plain, apart from makers' marks and the occasional circular raised pad where an ejector pin had pushed the piece out of its mould after casting. Due to manufacturers' variations and the declining fortunes of Germany after 1942 the finishes applied to

Third Reich belt buckles ranged from gold plate, silver plate and enamel to white and gilt washes and silver paint. Many of the latest kriegsmetall examples were issued in their natural slate grey.

With such a variety among original buckles, the one common denominator was high quality. The RZM strictly supervised the manufacture of all NSDAP related pieces and the competition for lucrative government contracts which existed among the vast number of authorised makers of non-Party buckles ensured that the appearance of these items, too, was never less than excellent. Indeed, production methods were on a par with those used in the decorations field.

Many varieties of fake buckle are on the market. Most original designs have been copied and completely fictitious 'prototypes' created, but none of these reproductions can match the crisp appearance of even the latest originals. The majority display poor detailing, indistinct pebbling, ungeometric swastikas and rough edges, and the RZM symbol, when present, is often in the form shown at (b) on **Fig 4**. Some spurious buckles simply comprise brass blanks with small civilian stick-pin badges or cap eagles roughly soldered or pinned into position. One particularly common 'fantasy' is stamped from nickel plated brass and features an SS 1934-pattern totenkopf.

The most convincing copies are cast in aluminium, with a hollow reverse, as illustrated in **Plates 177** and **178**. These generally have a blistered obverse surface but their main point of identification is that they have a fragile 'C'-shaped catch soldered into position on the reverse. The original 'C'-shaped catch was restricted to steel and some brass buckles, but was never used on aluminium examples because of the brazing difficulties with lightweight metal.

During the 1970s a large number of fakes, including the one shown in **Plate 179**, were stamped from rusted steel, so rust should not in itself be taken as a sign of authenticity. Happily, these steel fakes, while appearing old, do not stand up to close inspection since their finish is rough and their detailing very poor. None would ever have passed the quality control inspectors in Third Reich factories.

Plate 176 Belt Buckles: *all original. This plate illustrates the reverse characteristics of each of the four main varieties of other ranks' belt buckle. The buckle at top left is an early stamped brass one featuring a plain finish, semi-circular 'depressed slot' catch, two soldering points and the first pattern 'post and prongs'. The buckle at top right is* die-struck aluminium with typical 'drilled protuberance' catch and second pattern 'post and prongs'. The item at centre is die-stamped steel, with 'C'-shaped catch affixed by brazing and leather tab or 'lederwiderhalt' to prevent slippage. The buckle at bottom is cast in heavy zinc-based kriegsmetall.

121

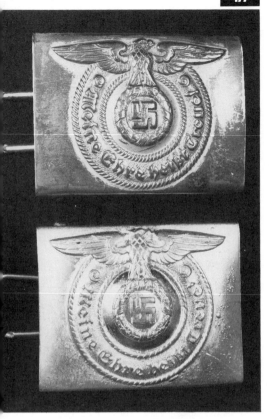

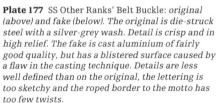

Plate 177 SS Other Ranks' Belt Buckle: *original (above) and fake (below). The original is die-struck steel with a silver-grey wash. Detail is crisp and in high relief. The fake is cast aluminium of fairly good quality, but has a blistered surface caused by a flaw in the casting technique. Details are less well defined than on the original, the lettering is too sketchy and the roped border to the motto has too few twists.*

Plate 178 *Reverse of items shown in* **Plate 177**. *The original is of wartime period manufacture and unmarked. The fake bears the spurious RZM and diamond-shaped SS proofmarks shown at (f) on* **Fig 4**, *accompanied by the code number 'OLT/ 62637', a combination totally unlike anything used during the Third Reich. (The earliest SS buckles were manufactured by the firm of Overhoff & Co, Lüdenscheid, and were stamped 'O & C Ges.Gesch.'. The 'OLT' on the reproduction may be an inaccurate rendering of the later Overhoff trademark, which was 'OLC' within a diamond.) Note that the fake has a 'C'-shaped catch soldered into position. This form of catch was never used on original aluminium buckles.*

Plate 179 *TeNo Other Ranks' Belt Buckle: reproduction. Regulations make no mention of any special belt buckle having existed for TeNo rank and file, who generally wore double claw open face buckles. This fake is therefore a postwar fantasy, with a central design based loosely on that of the circular belt buckle used by TeNo officers. It has been crudely stamped from rusted steel, giving it an 'old' appearance even when new. The eagle is deformed, its head faces in the wrong direction, and the surrounding wreath is of oakleaves instead of laurel leaves.*

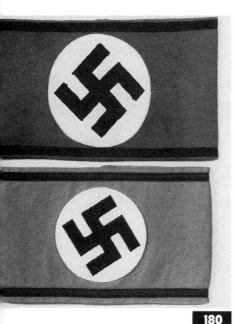

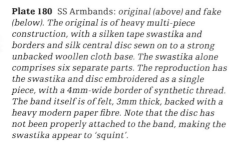

180

181

182

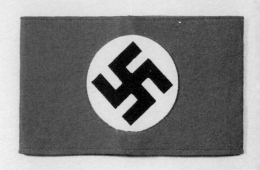

Plate 180 SS Armbands: *original (above) and fake (below). The original is of heavy multi-piece construction, with a silken tape swastika and borders and silk central disc sewn on to a strong unbacked woollen cloth base. The swastika alone comprises six separate parts. The reproduction has the swastika and disc embroidered as a single piece, with a 4mm-wide border of synthetic thread. The band itself is of felt, 3mm thick, backed with a heavy modern paper fibre. Note that the disc has not been properly attached to the band, making the swastika appear to 'squint'.*

Plate 181 NSDAP Armband: *original. This item is silk-screen printed on linen. It is affixed to the sleeve by four small cotton loops along the upper side.*

Plate 182 NSDAP Armband: *fake. The swastika and disc are embroidered as a single piece, with a synthetic thread border. The felt band is backed with paper fibre.*

123

Plate 183 Wartime Emergency Armbands: *original (above) and reproduction (below). The original is the regulation printed linen armband worn by members of the Volkssturm from October 1944. Ultimately, a number of unofficial variations on this design were manufactured. The reproduction is the so-called 'ersatz NSDAP armband', printed* on canvas sacking only 50mm in width and allegedly used in lieu of the standard Party armband during the closing months of the war. It is, in fact, a postwar fantasy, mass-produced for the American market in the 1960s.

Plate 184 *Reverse of items shown in* **Plate 183**.

ARMBANDS

Armbands were used for a variety of purposes during the Third Reich, notably to indicate the wearer's membership of a particular organisation, to show his function or office, and, in the case of the NSDAP, to denote his level of responsibility.

Armband colours, sizes and lettering styles differed considerably. The best examples were of multi-piece construction, with silken tape and/or bullion thread sewn on to a heavy woollen cloth or lightweight linen base to form the appropriate design. Others were hand-embroidered in bullion thread on wool, machine-embroidered in cotton thread on wool, cotton or linen, or machine-woven in cotton and/or silken threads. Silk-screen printing on cotton or linen was widely used in the production of standard NSDAP swastika armbands and regulation Volkssturm examples. By the end of the war, makeshift emergency armbands were being hand-stencilled in paint or waterproof ink on any scrap material available.

The faking of armbands has been restricted to the swastika armband and its derivatives, which are constantly in great demand. Fake bands are commonly in thick felt, either unbacked or backed with a modern heavy red paper fibre. The swastika and disc are typically machine-embroidered as a single piece, with a wide border of synthetic thread. Printed reproductions also circulate, on canvas rather than the correct wool, cotton or linen.

Plates 180 to **184** illustrate a selection of original and fake swastika armbands.

GORGETS

Original Nazi gorgets and chains of all types were produced variously in brass, tombak, German silver, steel and zinc with finishes ranging from fine enamel to rough paintwork. Gorget plates were expertly die-struck or cast with smooth semi-rolled edges, and the finely detailed obverse insignia on each was affixed by round pins or flat prongs pushed through holes in the plate and then bent over. The gorget reverse was backed by heavy woollen cloth or stiff card, and the maker's mark was occasionally stamped into one of the rear prongs.

The 'Feldgendarmerie', 'Feldjägerkorps', 'Bahnhofswache' and 'Zugwache' gorgets have been extensively copied. Their fake gorget plates are generally of very thin lightweight aluminium, which can easily be bent by hand. The edges are unrolled and poorly finished, and insignia is often blurred in places and glued into position. The reproduction backing is usually of felt, or a shiny PVC-type paper, and the central rear prongs are too wide and bear spurious RZM or DRGM marks. **Plates 185** and **186** compare original and reproduction gorgets.

DAY BADGES

Tens of millions of so-called 'day badges' were produced and sold on the open market during the Third Reich to commemorate and partly finance Party Days, sports meetings, paramilitary events, cultural occasions and so on. Materials used in their manufacture included copper, brass, tombak, German silver, aluminium, tin, zinc, plastic and even leather and cardboard, but quality was kept consistently high. **Plates 187** and **188** illustrate a small selection of originals.

The vast number of genuine day badges still circulating has, until now, precluded the need for reproduction. However, with the constantly decreasing availability and increasing prices of even the most common Nazi medals and awards, more and more young collectors are specialising in day

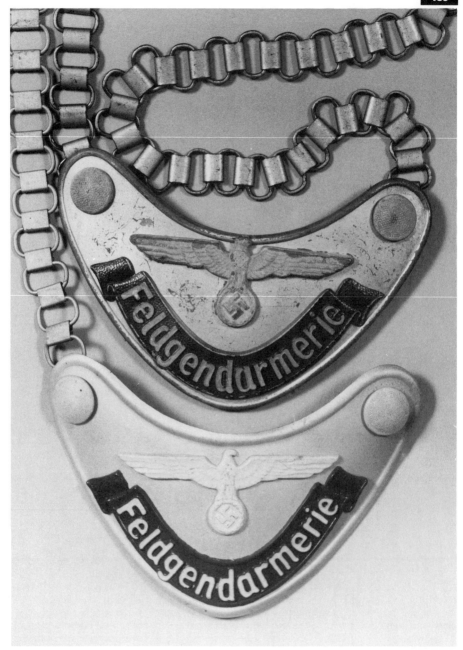

Plate 185 Feldgendarmerie Gorget: *original (above) and fake (below). The original gorget plate is stamped from heavy sheet steel with smooth semi-rolled edges. The chain links are also in silver painted steel. The fake plate and chain are in lightweight aluminium, which can easily be bent by hand. The edges of the plate are rough and poorly finished.*

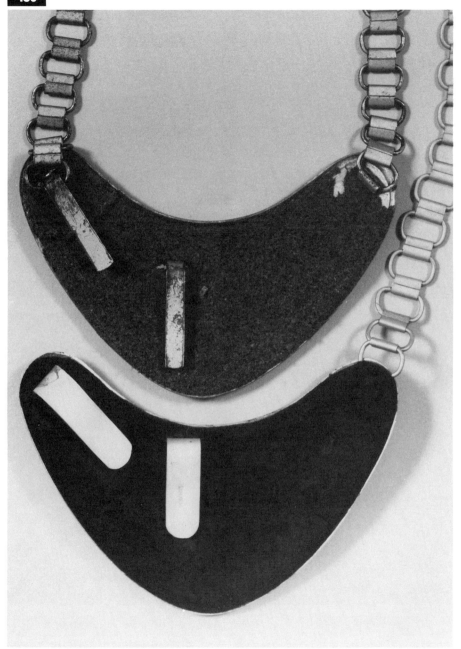

Plate 186 *Reverse of items shown in* **Plate 185**. *The original (above) is backed with field grey woollen cloth and the narrow prongs are unmarked. The fake (below) has a black felt backing and its prongs are noticeably wider than those on the original. The central prong is stamped 'DRGM'.*

127

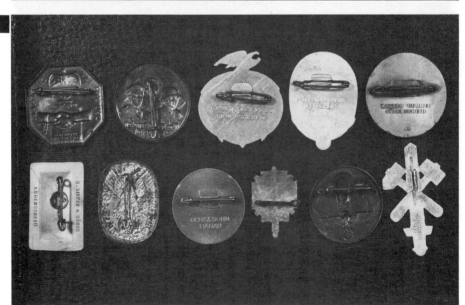

Plate 187 Day Badges: *all original. This photograph illustrates a small selection of commemorative and donation badges to show their consistent high quality. Some are cast, others die-stamped, and materials used in their manufacture include brass, tombak, tin, aluminium and zinc. The badge at lower left is in grey plastic.*

Plate 188 *Reverse of items shown in* **Plate 187**. *Note that each is smoothly finished with a common pin assembly. Those with solid backs are maker marked.*

128

badges and it is only a matter of time before the demand for them makes their faking a worthwhile proposition. Until then, col-lectors can continue to buy with confidence attractive pieces which are sure to prove worthwhile long-term investments.

FLAGS & PENNANTS

Nazi Germany produced a huge quantity of assorted flags, banners and pennants, all of which are highly collectable and widely faked. Original examples of the three most commonly used flags, ie the National War Flag (see **Plate 189**), the National Service Flag and the Swastika Flag, may be found in a variety of sizes and qualities, some being of double-sided multi-piece cotton construc-tion, but the majority being of printed canvas with the reverse showing a 'mirror' image of the obverse design. Each bore a halyard rope along the hoist edge, held in place by a white cotton or linen strip which was usually stamped in black ink with the flag's designation, its size in metres and, sometimes, a maker's mark. Fakes are typically printed on linen and are generally deformed, with ill-proportioned eagles, swastikas and Iron Crosses (see **Plate 190**). They usually lack the halyard rope and the hoist edge is often of a white synthetic material and unmarked (see **Plate 191**). Many reproductions are also characterised by poor dyeing techniques resulting in wrong colour shading, some even having orange fields instead of red and yellow areas where there should be white.

The earliest Nazi vehicle pennants were hand-stitched affairs, often crude in form, produced locally for political and para-military leaders (see **Plate 192**). From 1935, however, by which time the RZM system was fully operational, NSDAP car pennants were made only by contracted professional firms, in hand-embroidery, machine-embroidery or BEVo weave. Military and civil pennants were also subject to stringent manufactur-ing controls. Most fakes are let down by their rough quality, ungeometric swastikas, pigeon-like eagles and so on. Others are quite convincing, but lack the metal wire stiffener or any other means of attaching pennant to vehicle (see **Plate 193**).

Original trumpet banners, drum covers and rostrum drapes were made variously from wool, linen, cotton, bullion thread, silk and velvet, depending upon the item involved. Fairly common pieces such as Hitler Youth trumpet banners (see **Plate 194**), for example, came in machine-stitched linen or cotton whereas Wehrmacht cere-monial items were in heavy silk. Most fakes simply do not have the professional finish of the real thing, or are let down by the fact that they are made from postwar shiny synthetic materials (see **Plates 195** and **196**). Above all, collectors should remember that natural oxidation causes both silver and gold bullion thread to tarnish through time and any such embroidery in mint condition may be viewed with at least a degree of suspicion.

WRITTEN DOCUMENTS

Nazi documents of all kinds are collectable, and almost every type has been copied. Those in greatest demand, and consequently the most widely faked, are the items signed by Hitler or one of the other Third Reich leaders. Specialist forgers in West Germany and the USA have recently made a full-time business out of counterfeiting the auto-graphs of Nazi personalities, often on original sheets of appropriately headed paper. Fakes of Hitler's signature, in par-ticular, abound, usually written on wartime postcards or photographs of the Führer. When examining such pieces, it is worth remembering that the only photographs of himself which Hitler signed for presentation

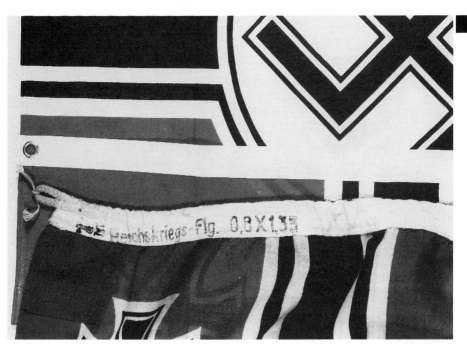

Plate 189 National War Flag: *original. This item is printed on canvas with the reverse showing a mirror image of the obverse design. It has a halyard rope along the hoist edge, held in place by a heavy white cotton strip.*

Plate 190 National War Flag: *fake. This printed linen reproduction was made in Taiwan in 1987. Its swastika is too thin, the disc and arms ill-proportioned and the Iron Cross deformed. The hoist edge bears a white synthetic strip with a small gilded tin ring at each end. There is no halyard rope.*

Plate 191 *Hoist edges of items shown in* **Plates 189** *and* **190**. *The reproduction (above) is plain while the original (below) is marked with the designation 'Reichskriegs-Flg.', size (in metres) '0.8 × 1.35' and naval issue stamp, all in black ink.*

Plate 192 NSKK Vehicle Pennant: *original. An early hand-produced chain-stitched example, manufactured around 1933 before RZM standardisation. It is double sided, with a metal wire stiffener which is stamped 'DRGM'. Later NSKK pennants were machine-embroidered or woven, with far superior detailing to the eagle.*

Plate 193 Traffic Police Vehicle Pennant: *reproduction. Machine-embroidered in red cotton on white with a red-and-white twisted silk border. There is no metal stiffener around the edge. The*

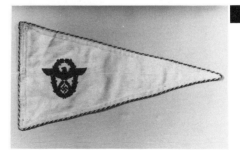

insignia is of a distinctive fake type from the same range as the reproduction Police arm eagle shown in **Plate 148**. *Nevertheless, this item would undoubtedly fool many collectors.*

131

Plate 194 Hitler Youth Fanfare Trumpet Banner: original. *This is a regulation item, in multi-piece cotton with white cotton fringes. The fanfare trumpet is standard HJ issue, by 'Colner'.*

Plate 195 Hitler Youth Fanfare Trumpet Banner: fake. *This reproduction is of excellent quality, featuring a multi-piece swastika and gold bullion fringe. The swastika is too small and the thin central white bar horizontal rather than vertical as in* **Plate 194**, *but these points are not in themselves sufficient to shed serious doubt upon the authenticity of the piece since there were a great*

many HJ banners produced during the early years of the Third Reich which did not conform to regulations. This item is conclusively exposed as a fake only by the fact that it is manufactured from a shiny synthetic nylon material, totally unlike anything made before 1945.

Plate 196 *Close-up of banners shown in* **Plates 194** *and* **195**. *The central diamond on the original (above) is attached to the banner cloth by means of a single row of cotton stitching whereas the fake diamond (below) has a 4mm-wide border of synthetic thread holding it in place.*

purposes were large studio portraits taken by his personal photographer, Heinrich Hoffmann. Any small signed photograph which does not bear the Hoffmann stamp should be regarded as suspect. **Plates 197** to **199** illustrate original and fake Hitler documents and **Fig 5** shows the changing styles of his signature.

It is difficult to give guidance in respect of other signed documents, since fakes are often comparable or even better in quality than the real thing (see **Plates 200** and **201**). It is safe to say that all wartime signatures should be in fountain pen ink, but many entirely genuine postwar autographs of former Third Reich leaders written in ball-point pen or felt-tipped pen also circulate widely (see **Plates 202** and **203**). In the final analysis, then, each collector must rely on his own 'gut feeling' with regard to signatures. He, and only he, must be fully satisfied that what he is getting is 'right'.

After autographs, award citations are the most eagerly sought-after pieces of Nazi paperwork. The more common citations, such as those illustrated in **Plates 204** to **206,** were carried by their recipients folded into the covers of the Soldbuch, or were filed inside the owner's Wehrpass at his unit HQ, so should always show signs of folding and wear. Printed copies are usually unfolded and too new looking. Numerous crude photocopies of blank citations have also been produced, with alleged recipients' details written or typed into place (see **Plate 207**).

Identity documents and passes have also been faked, but always differ in some detail from the originals (see **Plates 208** and **209**). Such copies tend to have photographs glued into place rather than being stapled or rivetted as on originals, and some British and American reproductions even feature elementary spelling mistakes in the German text. Many fake SS documents and passes have been typed using surviving SS typewriters such as the one illustrated in **Plates 210** and **211**, and even spurious rubber stamps have been made to 'authenticate' bogus paperwork (see **Plates 212** to **214**).

Wartime press negatives have been used to produce a vast quantity of photographic prints of Nazi leaders, troops at the front line, and so on. However, these prints are instantly recognisable as modern copies

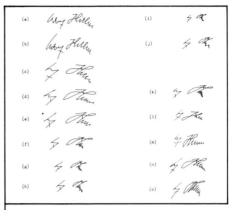

Fig 5 Changing Styles of Hitler's Signature: *original and fake. Hitler's handwriting, like that of most people, altered over the years as his fortunes and personality changed. These drawings show the various original styles of his signature, together with a few known fake examples.*

(a) original, November 1923.
(b) original, October 1925.
(c) original, March 1933.
(d) original, January 1937.
(e) original, July 1940.
(f) original, May 1941.
(g) original, January 1944.
(h) original, August 1944.
(i) original, December 1944.
(j) original, March 1945.
(k) fake, often encountered on reproduction signed photographs emanating from New Jersey, USA. Note the regular strokes of 'itler', not characteristic of any of the original styles.
(l) fake, found on spurious handwritten Hitler letters produced in West Germany.
(m) fake, seen on signed photographs made in the UK.
(n) fake, from the bogus Hitler Diaries of 1982.
(o) fake, also from the Hitler Diaries.

since they do not bear the war correspondent's stamp and official stencilled caption on the reverse, common to originals (see **Plate 215**).

A large number of Third Reich manufacturers' catalogues have been reprinted, but these are intended to assist researchers and collectors rather than to deceive. They usually include details of the reprint date and the modern publishing company responsible. **Plate 216** illustrates one of the best facsimile catalogues currently on the market, that of F. W. Assmann & Söhne, Lüdenscheid.

BERLIN, DEN 1. Januar 1937

SS Oberführer Ulrich Graf

Ihre mir anläßlich des Jahreswechsels
übermittelten Glückwünsche haben mich sehr
erfreut.
　　Ich erwidere Ihre Wünsche mit herz-
lichem Dank.

Plate 197 Adolf Hitler New Year Greeting Card: original. The signature is a facsimile, printed in blue on the card. Such items were mass-produced as a medium through which the Führer could thank all those who sent him their best wishes each New Year.

Plate 198 Autographed Presentation Copy of *Mein Kampf*: fake. The book itself is entirely original, and is one of the special leather-bound jubilee editions produced in 1939, the year of Hitler's 50th birthday. The autographed dedication, however, is faked, being an exact copy of Hitler's handwriting taken from an original presentation inscription. It was produced by the author to illustrate the point that just because a document is original, the writing upon it need not be. There is no doubt that this piece would fool many collectors — if they were careless enough to fail to notice that Hitler had addressed the book to a certain 'Herr Lumsden'!

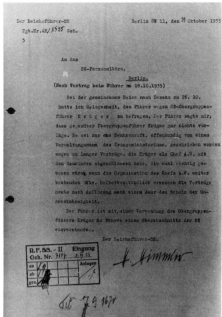

199

201

Plate 199 *Original leather binding of item shown in* **Plate 198**.

Plate 200 Heinrich Himmler Document: *original.* This secret internal memorandum, confirming the suitability of SS-Obergruppenführer Friedrich-Wilhelm Krüger to command an SS District, is signed by the Reichsführer-SS, Heinrich Himmler, in black ink. The SS Personnel Office red stamp of receipt can be clearly seen at the lower left of the page.

Plate 201 Heinrich Himmler Document: *fake.* This citation for the Anti-Partisan War Badge in gold to an SS-Sturmbannführer in the 7th SS-Mountain Division 'Prinz Eugen' is in the correct format for a late war temporary award certificate and corresponds with details in the official SS officers list. However, it was typed in 1988 on an aged fly-leaf page carefully removed from an old book, using the typewriter illustrated in **Plate 210**. Himmler's signature was traced from a modern textbook and the hand stamp, which was a naval one, deliberately smudged so that its inscription could not be read. The whole thing was then folded several times. A very convincing piece that took just 15min to produce.

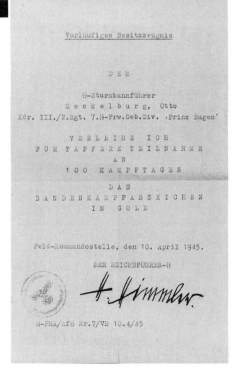

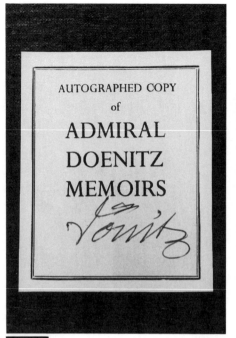

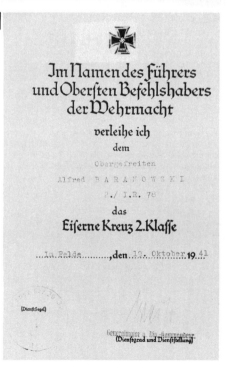

Plate 202 Admiral Dönitz Document: *original.*
Removed from a signed copy of Dönitz's postwar
memoirs, this label bears a genuine example of the
Admiral's autograph in blue ballpoint ink.

Plate 203 Admiral Dönitz Document: *fake. This*
realistic reproduction citation for the Naval
Combat Clasp was produced in the same way as
the item illustrated in **Plate 201**.

Plate 204 Citation: *original. A standard printed*
and typed citation for the Iron Cross Second Class,
signed in ink by the commander of the
26th Infantry Division.

BESITZZEUGNIS

DEM   Unteroffizier
(DIENSTGRAD)

Alfred B a r a n o w s k i
(VOR. UND FAMILIENNAME)

2. Kompanie Grenadier - Regiment 78
(TRUPPENTEIL)

VERLEIHE ICH FÜR TAPFERE TEILNAHME
AN   15   NAHKAMPFTAGEN

DIE   1. STUFE DER
NAHKAMPFSPANGE

Rgt.Gef.Stand, den 19. Mai 1944
(ORT UND DATUM)

(STEMPEL)   (UNTERSCHRIFT)

Oberst und Rgt.Kommandeur.
(DIENSTGRAD UND DIENSTSTELLUNG)

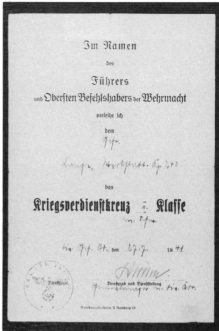

Im Namen

des

Führers

und Obersten Befehlshabers der Wehrmacht

verleihe ich

dem

das

Kriegsverdienstkreuz 2. Klasse
m. Schw.

den 27.7.   19 41

Dienstsiegel   Dienstgrad und Dienststellung

Wehrkreisdrukerei X Hamburg 13

207

206

In Anerkennung seiner Verdienste
um die Deutschland übertragenen
Olympischen Spiele 1936
verleihe ich dem

Reichsführer-ﬀ
Heinrich HIMMLER

das
Deutsche Olympia-Ehrenzeichen
erster Klasse.

Berlin, den   30. Januar   1937

Der Deutsche Reichskanzler

Plate 205 Citation: *original. A standard printed and typed citation for the Close Combat Clasp in Bronze, signed in ink by the commander of the 78th Grenadier Regiment.*

Plate 206 Citation: *original. A printed and handwritten citation for the War Merit Cross Second Class with Swords, signed in indelible pencil by the commander of the 170th Infantry Division.*

Plate 207 Citation: *fake. This item, for the Olympic Games Decoration First Class, is one of a series of crude photocopies of blank originals with award dates and recipients' names typed in. They have all been produced on ordinary typing paper, totally unlike the quality vellum used on the real thing. This particular piece is named to Heinrich Himmler but ends with Hitler's title, 'Der Deutsche Reichskanzler' ('German Chancellor'), which was used only on Olympic Games Citations presented to foreigners. Those given to German recipients referred to Hitler as 'Der Führer und Reichskanzler'.*

Plate 208 Army Wehrpass: *original (left) and fake (right). The issued original is in heavy green card with horizontal ridges and a linen spine. The reproduction is of very high quality, but with vertical ridges and a thin paper spine. The gothic lettering style used on the fake was also featured on early originals, so cannot be used as an indicator when deciding authenticity. Both pieces bear the maker's mark of Metten & Co, Berlin.*

Plate 209 *Interior of items shown in* **Plate 208**. *Note that the eagle printed in the centre of the page on the original (above) has a dark swastika on a light background. That on the fake (below) has a light swastika on a dark background.*

Almost every sundry item of Nazi regalia which was produced before 1945, including identity discs, wall plaques and dress rings, has been reproduced since then. As a rule of thumb, originals tend to be of good quality and show signs of age while fakes are inferior in construction and too new looking. **Plates 217** and **220** show typical examples.

Plate 210 SS Typewriter: *original. Typewriters with special runic keys were introduced during the first half of 1936 for use in SS offices. This portable example bears the mark of a Dutch retailer but was reputedly 'liberated' by a British officer from Buchenwald Concentration Camp in 1945.*

Presumably, the original owner was transferred from Holland to the camp, taking his typewriter with him. Such machines are now very rare, and worth their weight in gold to the faker who can use them to produce authentic-looking 'SS documents' such as that illustrated in **Plate 201**.

Plate 211 *Close-up of the runic key featured on the typewriter shown in* **Plate 210**.

Plate 212 Document Stamp: *original. This piece has a brown wooden handle and circular stainless steel base, typical of wartime stamps. The inscription reads 'Kriegsmarine - Marinebefehlshaber', indicating that it was used at the office of a local naval commander.*

Plate 213 Document Stamp: *reproduction. One of a range of fake stamps made to authenticate bogus documents. All have black wooden handles and square or rectangular Perspex and rubber bases. This one bears the legend 'Panz. Abt. 507' and refers to a Tiger tank battalion formed in September 1943, which fought its entire war on the eastern front.*

Plate 214 RZM Label Stamp: *reproduction. This item (right), from the same range of stamps as that illustrated in* **Plate 213**, *was made to produce fake RZM labels. The formation of the RZM symbol on the stamp is clearly inaccurate, but in any case all original RZM labels were printed, not rubber-stamped. An original label (left) is shown for comparison purposes.*

Plate 215 Reverse of Press Photograph: *original. The stamp at top right is that of the SS war correspondent responsible for release of the photograph to the German Press. The stencilled label at centre is the official caption authorised to accompany the picture. All original Press photographs should be marked like this on the back.*

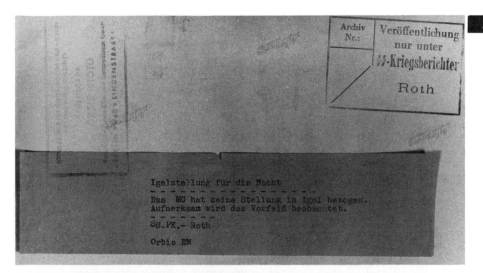

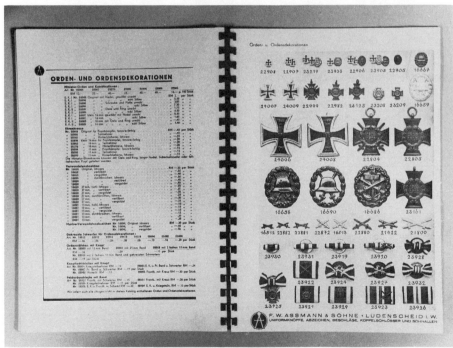

Plate 216 Manufacturer's Catalogue: reproduction. All commercial makers of insignia, decorations, edged weapons and other Third Reich military accoutrements issued sales catalogues advertising their wares and many of these have now been reprinted for the benefit of researchers and collectors. That illustrated is a modern copy of 'Der Assmannkatalog', produced by the firm of F. W. Assmann & Söhne, Lüdenscheid. Reprints such as this are not intended to deceive, and can be of great assistance as they often show in detail regulation sizes, styles and metals used, as well as contemporary wholesale and retail prices.

Plate 217 Identity Discs: *originals (top and bottom left) and fake (bottom right). The original at top is a standard military 'dog tag' in die-stamped zinc. It was worn by a member of the 1st SS-Totenkopf Standarte and bears his regimental number '672' and blood group 'A'. The original at bottom left is also stamped zinc, and was issued to Prisoner-of-War No 16614 incarcerated in the PoW camp at Thorn. The fake at bottom right is a poor quality reproduction of a Gestapo warrant disc, in cast white metal alloy, with an edge seam. Original Gestapo discs were die-struck from brass or German silver.*

Plate 218 Waffen-SS Motorcycle Registration Plate: *original. This piece is painted on sheet steel and is heavily rusted, scored and pitted. It illustrates the sort of genuine 'weathering' which no amount of artificial distressing by the faker can achieve.*

Plate 219 Sugar Bowl: *original. This high quality item is produced in German silver plate and bears an embossed national emblem flanked by the initials 'DR'. Pieces so marked are frequently offered for sale as rare tableware from the senior officers' mess of the SS Division 'Das Reich'. They are, in fact, fairly common and merely graced the dining carriages on trains of the 'Deutsche Reichsbahn', the German national railway system.*

142

BIBLIOGRAPHY

It has not been possible to provide a list of books devoted entirely to the field of Third Reich fake detection, since this is the first comprehensive work on the subject to be published. However, the books mentioned below may be of some limited assistance to collectors seeking to determine the authenticity of prospective purchases or of items already in their possession.

Unfortunately, almost every reference volume dealing with Nazi regalia, no matter how scholarly and expensive, includes at least a few photographs of readily available reproduction items to supplement those of originals in illustrating the text. This is a positively confusing and misleading state of affairs, for only a small number of authors have made any effort to identify the fakes which they have used for illustrative purposes as such and, even when the distinction is made, there tends to be little or no description of what the real thing should look like.

Angolia, J. R. — For Führer and Fatherland Vols 1 & 2: *Military, Political and Civil Awards of the Third Reich*. (Bender, California 1976-78). Vol 1 includes a short section on post war production, but it should be noted that in each volume several photographs which purport to be of original items are, in fact, of fakes.

Baer, L. — *The History of the German Steel Helmet, 1916-1945*. (Bender, California 1985). Many excellent photographs of original helmet variants with particularly good coverage of genuine decals and the techniques used to apply them.

Borsarello, J. and Lassus, D. — *Camouflaged Uniforms of the Waffen-SS*, Vols 1 & 2, (Iso-Galago, London, 1986-88). Comprehensive colour illustrations of all the original Waffen-SS camouflage patterns, and notes on the wartime construction layout for the camouflage smock.

Bowen, V. E. — *The Prussian and German Iron Cross*, (Iron Cross Research Publi-cations, England 1986). Superb coverage of the methods used to produce Third Reich and Federal Iron Crosses and associated awards.

Catella, F. — *Waffenfabrik Katalog*, (RZM Publications, Strasbourg 1986). Reprints of the sales catalogues issued by the principal German edged weapon and badge manufacturers between 1920 and 1945. Vividly illustrates many original swords, daggers, metal insignia, and other accoutrements, with makers' variants, official regulations governing production and wear, and wartime prices. French and German text.

Hamilton, C. — *Leaders and Personalities of the Third Reich*, (Bender, California 1984). Illustrates photographs of original examples of the autographs of most Nazi leaders, useful for comparing with signatures on suspect documents.

Klietmann, K. G. — *Auszeichnungen des Deutschen Reiches, 1936-1945*, (Motòrbuch Verlag, Stuttgart 1982). Includes frontal photos of a few fake Third Reich awards, which are so described. German text.

McFarlane, R. — *Bluebook of Identification of Reproduction Nazi Edged Weapons*, (Published privately, Oxford 1969). A very basic and outdated pamphlet.

McGuirk, D. — *Rommel's Army in Africa*, (Stanley Paul, London 1987). Excellent colour photographs showing many original variants, both official and unofficial, of Afrikakorps uniform items.

Shutt, T. — *Dress and Field Service Hats of the Third Reich*, (HSM Publications, Missouri 1981). Includes brief verbal coverage of reproduction peaked caps.

SS-Personalhauptamt. — *Dienstaltersliste der Schutzstaffel der NSDAP: Reichsführer-SS — SS-Sturmbannführer*,

(INFORA Research Establishment, Liechtenstein 1985). Reprint of the SS Senior Officers List of 9 November 1944, detailing name, date of birth, rank, unit, Party No, SS No, decorations etc, for each of the 5,500 serving SS officers from SS-Sturmbannführer upwards. Invaluable reference for cross-checking details shown on suspect SS letters, citations, and other documents. German text.

Stephens, F. J. — *Reproduction? Recognition!* (Militaria Collector Inc, California 1981). A finely researched work, but restricted to the detection of fake Nazi daggers.

Stewart, E. C. — *Wehrpasses and Soldbuchs*, (Published privately, Ohio 1985). Illustrates many original Wehrpasses and Soldbuchs, with interesting variations in Sütterlin script handwriting and unit stamps.

Williamson, G. — *The Iron Cross*, (Blandford, Poole 1984). Includes a brief section on fake Iron Crosses.

220

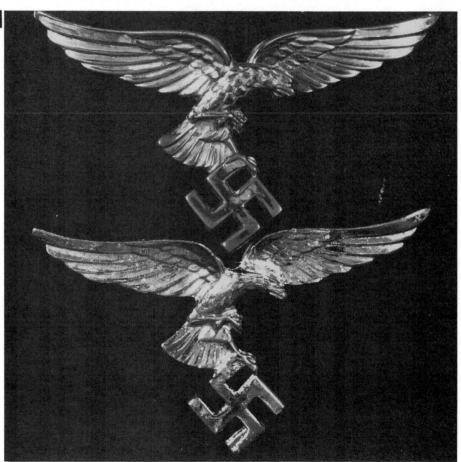

Plate 220 Luftwaffe Plaque Eagles: *original (above) and fake (below). The original is in hollow cast silver plated zinc, with two screws on the reverse, and was removed from an example of the*

1942 Plaque for Outstanding Achievement in Luftgau XI. The reproduction is in solid cast glittery white metal with an unstable needle pin assembly soldered to the rear.